Monographic Journals of the Near East   *Assur* 4/1 (March 1984)

KHABUR WARE AND N
THEIR ORIGIN, RELATIONSHIP,

Diana L. Stein

Khabur Ware and Nuzi Ware are two types of painted pottery in northern Mesopotamia during the second millennium B.C. which have hitherto been treated independently of their respective archaeological contexts on the basis of their painted decoration. Both categories of painted wares were regarded as intrusive and were accordingly attributed to intrusive peoples – namely, the Hurrians.

The present study reviews the evidence for Khabur Ware and Nuzi Ware and examines the stratigraphic sequence at a number of key sites in north Mesopotamia and north Syria from the viewpoint of a wider Syro-Mesopotamian frame in order to determine the extent to which these two pottery categories were intrusive and that to which they were indigenous. The resulting modifications of the conventional Khabur Ware and Nuzi Ware classifications show that while these two wares are quite distinct from each other in terms of origin, function, date, and distribution, neither category of painted pottery is entirely unprecedented in Mesopotamia and, neither, therefore, can be representative of intrusive peoples. Although the distinction in date and distribution between Khabur Ware and Nuzi Ware may reflect changing spheres of political and commercial contacts, the discrepancy between the function of these two wares precludes the same explanation for their origin. Only Nuzi Ware may be conceived as a product of political and economic conditions.

Table of Contents

[1] The present study is a revised version of an MA thesis submitted in 1979 to the Institute of Archaeology of the University of London. I am grateful to Professor D. Oates for encouraging this research, and I would particularly like to thank both Professor E. Porada and Dr. P.R.S. Moorey for their helpful comments and suggested improvements upon the original manuscript.

Abbreviations

AAAS	*Annales Archéologiques Arabes Syriennes*
AJA	*American Journal of Archaeology*
BASOR	*Bulletin of the American Schools of Oriental Research*
Belleten	*Türk Tarih Kurumu Belleten*
CAH	*Cambridge Ancient History*
IEJ	*Israel Exploration Journal*

JAOS	*Journal of the American Oriental Society*
JCS	*Journal of Cuneiform Studies*
JESHO	*Journal of the Economic and Social History of the Orient*
JNES	*Journal of Near Eastern Studies*
LAAA	*Liverpool Annals of Anthropology and Archaeology*
MDP	*Mémoires de la Délégation en Perse*
OIP	*Oriental Institute Publication*, University of Chicago
Rev. Hittite	*Revue Hittite et Asianique*
UE	*Joint Expedition of the British Museum and of the Museum of the University of Pennsylvania. Ur Excavations*
UE II	Woolley, C.L., *The Royal Cemetery* (1934)
UE VII	Woolley, C.L. and Mallowan, M., *The Old Babylonian Period* (1976)
UE VIII	Woolley, C.L., *The Kassite Period and the Period of the Assyrian Kings* (1965)
WVDOG	*Wissenschaftliche Veröffentlichungen der Deutschen Orient-Gessellschaft*

1. Introduction

The identification of a material culture with an ethnic group is now regarded with scepticism, if not altogether discouraged (Mellink:1972-5, 514-519; Hamlin:1971; Kramer:1977), and the instability of such an equation has been discussed at length in two recent publications of collected essays devoted entirely to the particular problems and pitfalls inherent in the definition of a Hurrian material culture based on the combined archaeological and linguistic evidence available to date (Barrelet:1977, *Rev. Hittite:* 1978). Many of the established hallmarks of Hurrian culture have been rejected, or at least discredited, as each was analyzed separately in its proper historical context. Thus, it has been found that some of the alleged Hurrian deities actually antedate the arrival of the Hurrians in northern Syria and Mesopotamia and have, therefore, been eliminated from the original Hurrian pantheon (Haas:1978). Similarly, several of the individual art works and elements of iconography previously attributed to the Hurrians appear to have roots in the earlier traditions of Anatolia and Mesopotamia and are no longer to be considered of Hurrian origin (Paraayre:1977). Most unsettling of all, perhaps, is the observation that Hurrian names, which in the past served as the primary evidence for reconstructing the existence and extent of a Hurrian population, were at times adopted by non-Hurrians as a result of fashion or political trends and, therefore, do not necessarily have ethnic associations (Durand:1977; Charpin:1977). The conclusions reached independently by these studies and summarized by Barrelet show overwhelmingly that it is almost impossible to relate a specific category of archaeological material to an ethnic sector of a composite population (Barrelet:1977, 10-11), particularly, one might add, when the specific categories themselves have not been adequately defined. This conclusion inevitably casts doubt upon all remaining attributes of Hurrian material culture that have not yet been or cannot be entirely dissociated from their ethnic ties.

Khabur Ware and Nuzi Ware are two such remaining suspect categories of Hurrian art which have hitherto eluded historical analysis. Until quite recently, in fact, both ceramic categories have been treated independently of their respective archaeological contexts on the basis of their painted decoration.

The term "Khabur Ware" was originally introduced by Mallowan to describe a large storage vessel distinguished by its matt painted monochrome decoration, consisting of horizontal bands and geometric motifs, which he found in considerable quantities in the Khabur valley. Mallowan's evolving definition and evaluation of Khabur Ware was formulated almost entirely on the basis of his discoveries at Chagar Bazar (Mallowan:1936; 1937; 1947), and eventually he included under the heading of Khabur Ware virtually all contemporary shapes and wares with some form of painted decoration. His broad classification was generally accepted as a point of departure for further studies on Khabur Ware, some of which sought to divide this ware into two inter-related subgroups, an "older" and a "younger" variety of Khabur Ware, on the basis of style and the little stratigraphic evidence that is available (Welker:1948, 209; Hrouda:1957, 22; Kantor in McEwan:1958, 22-23).

The "younger" variety, consisting by and large of smaller, more delicately made vases and cups with banded decoration and occasional animal motifs, is considered in some respects to be transitional between the "older" Khabur Ware and another painted pottery style known as Nuzi Ware (Ibid.).

The term "Nuzi Ware" was proposed by Mallowan (1946) after the archaeological site where this distinctive white on dark painted pottery was first found in an archaeological context. It had originally been called "Hurrian Ware" by Speiser, who associated this pottery with an ethno-linguistic group of the same name (Speiser:1933a, 274). To avoid a racial nomenclature, Mallowan initially suggested that it rather be called "Subartu Pottery" after a geographic designation which, in the early Akkadian period, referred to the northern country between the Zagros and the Lebanese mountains which corresponded roughly to the distribution of this pottery (Mallowan:1939). Later, however, following the criticism that an Akkadian term erroneously implied a date earlier than the second millennium B.C. for the appearance of the white painted pottery, Mallowan abandoned "Subartu Pottery" in favor of "Nuzi Ware". An alternate, though less frequently adopted name for the same pottery is "Mitannian Ware", introduced by O'Callaghan in order to emphasize the similar date and distribution of the pottery and the Mitannian confederacy (O'Callaghan:1948, 72).

Khabur Ware was considered by Mallowan and others to be intrusive in north Mesopotamia due to the absence of painted decoration in the earlier levels of the limited area excavated at Chagar Bazar. The origin of this ware was thus sought through parallels in the well established traditions of painted ceramics of neighboring regions such as those of Iran and Syria (see below 3.4.1.).

The "younger" Khabur Ware was derived from the "older" Khabur Ware, although the occasional decoration of animal and figural motifs was taken to reflect a new foreign element whose origin was traced alternately to prototypes in the painted wares of Iran and to Bichrome Ware of Palestine (see below 2.3.2; 3.4.1).

Nuzi Ware, on account of its high technical quality and the absence of obvious precursors for its distinctive white painted decoration, was likewise regarded as intrusive in north Mesopotamia later in the mid-second millennium B.C. Similarities between Nuzi Ware and the "younger" Khabur Ware have been mentioned, but the many parallels between the painted designs of Nuzi Ware and various forms of decoration in Egypt, the Levant, and the Aegean encouraged some scholars to propose a western origin for it (see 3.4.2).

In accordance with contemporary theories of cultural change, the successive appearance of Khabur Ware and Nuzi Ware were attributed to intrusive peoples. First Nuzi Ware, and then Khabur Ware as well, were taken to be archaeological indicators of different penetrations into the Near East by the Hurrians. The lines of argument differed in each case. For Nuzi Ware, there was the evidence provided by associated inscriptions on tablets from stratum II at Nuzi itself (Speiser:1933a, 274; Mallowan:1946, 132; Hrouda:1957, 44). The chronology of Nuzi became central to the dating of the stratigraphy at other sites where levels containing Nuzi Ware were designated as Hurrian (Brak levels 2-1, Mallowan: 1947; Billa stratum 3, Speiser:1933a; Chagar Bazar level 1e, Mallowan:1947, 83) and dated either earlier or later than Nuzi stratum II, depending upon the direction from which the Hurrians are believed to have entered northern Mesopotamia.

Khabur Ware, in particular the "younger" variety, was then indirectly attributed to the Hurrians through Nuzi Ware with which it shared the same stratigraphic context at a number of sites (Billa 3, Brak 3 and 2, Jidle 2, Chagar Bazar Ie, and Alalakh IV). Mallowan implied a common cultural source for both of these two painted wares when he suggested that certain features of the "younger" variety of Khabur Ware may have been influenced by the white on black painted Nuzi Ware of the Hurrians (Mallowan: 1937, 102; 1947, 239). The identification of Khabur Ware with the Hurrians was promoted by Welker in her survey of the third and second millennium B.C. pottery of the Near East (1948, 218). It was later modified by Hrouda in a similar study based on the second millennium B.C. painted pottery from Assur, in which he suggests that Khabur Ware is cognate to the painted pottery of north Syria ("Syrian painted ware" of Cilicia and the Amuq[2] and Anatolia ("Intermediate Ware")[3], and he reasoned deductively that if the Hurrians were to be equated with Khabur Ware, then they would also have to be connected with the introduction of painted decoration in Anatolia during the latter part of the third millenium B.C.

Hrouda, however, refutes the Hurrian connection either with painted pottery in general or, by association with Khabur Ware, in particular, on the grounds that painted pottery appears comparatively late in northern Mesopotamia, the alleged homeland of the Hurrians, and that contemporary painted pottery is altogether absent from regions in southern Mesopotamia where textual sources record the presence of Hurrians from the Ur III period onwards (Hrouda:1957, 43-45). He proposed instead, that Hurrian influence be seen in the animal and figural motifs which seem to appear at a later stage in the development of painted pottery both in northern Syria and northern Mesopotamia and which, according to Hrouda, reflect a specific ethnic characteristic (1957, 44). In his review of Hrouda's monograph, Deshayes dismisses the arguments against associating the introduction of painted pottery in Anatolia and Syria with the Hurrians. He explains the

[2] The term "Syrian Painted Ware" was introduced by M.V. Seton-Williams (1953,57f.) in reference to the jugs and carinated bowls with painted triglyph-metope decoration which are indigenous to northern Syria and Cilicia.

[3] "Intermediate Ware" was first recognized at Alishar in levels 7M-6M (Osten, H.H., von der, *The Alishar Hüyük. OIP* 28:1937,236).

late appearance of painted pottery in north Mesopotamia by postulating the existence of unfavorable political conditions preceding the fall of the Ur III Dynasty which prevented Hurrian penetration into this region during their initial westward migration from Iran to Anatolia. He attributes the absence of contemporary painted pottery in southern Mesopotamia to the fact that the Hurrian component of the local southern population was insignificant (Deshayes:1959, 123). Deshayes is careful, on the one hand, to point out that it is not possible to prove a correlation between the Hurrians and animal representations on painted pottery. This observation does not discourage him from concluding, on the other hand, that the late third to early second millennium B.C. painted pottery of the Near East is a Hurrian phenomenon (Deshayes:1959, 124). The Hurrian connection was, thus, extended backwards from its original association with Nuzi Ware in the mid-second millennium B.C. to Khabur Ware in the early second millennium B.C., and thence, via Syrian painted pottery, to the Intermediate Ware of Anatolia in the late third millennium B.C.

The widely divergent interpretations and derivations of Khabur Ware and Nuzi Ware suggest that neither category has been clearly defined. Khabur Ware, if narrowly defined, as in Mallowan's initial description, means little more than storage jars with matt painted bands and is too general to be a useful analytical tool. If more broadly conceived, as in Mallowan's later work and that of all subsequent commentators, Khabur Ware has come to embrace a wide range of shapes, wares, and painted patterns which have little other than dark matt paint in common. Nuzi Ware is defined primarily in terms of its white painted design and only secondarily in terms of its shape and fabric so that as a result, many very similar, even identical wares and shapes without white painted decoration are automatically excluded from this category. Those instances where Khabur Ware and Nuzi Ware overlap - as for example dark paint on a typical Nuzi shape, or white paint on a Khabur Ware shape - defy categorization under the given terms and have, thus, led to confusion. After almost a century of use, neither term may be casually discarded, but it is increasingly vital that they should be defined and used with due regard to their character as modified by new evidence or by fresh appraisals of early evidence in the light of new finds.

The first attempt to relate one of these painted groups to its archaeological setting concerns an analysis of Khabur Ware in the context of its associated ceramic assemblage at Dinkha Tepe in the Azerbaijan (Hamlin:1971; Hamlin:1974). The site, however, lies well outside the main area of Khabur Ware distribution in northern Mesopotamia, and the absence of many wares associated with, and including north Mesopotamian types of Khabur Ware from Dinkha Tepe, suggests that its assemblage represents only a limited phase of Khabur Ware and, therefore, does not provide the historical development needed to evaluate this particular pottery.

The present study is concerned with the grouping of Khabur Ware and Nuzi Ware, and its purpose is primarily the historical development of both categories of painted pottery. By examining the stratigraphic sequence at a number of key sites and by placing their ceramic repertory in the wider Syro-Mesopotamian frame, I have sought to show the extent to which these two pottery categories were intrusive, and that to which they were indigenous. The resulting modifications in the conventional groupings of Khabur Ware and Nuzi Ware inevitably imply certain conclusions about the standard interpretations of the Hurrian connection, but only incidentally.

2.   Review of Sites

The earliest discoveries of "Khabur Ware" and "Nuzi Ware" took place at much the same time as American teams excavated at Nuzi, modern Yorgan Tepe (1925-1931) and Tell Billa (1930-1934) in Iraq and a British team, under Mallowan, worked successively at Chagar Bazar (1935-1937) and Tell Brak (1937-1938) in northeast Syria. The work was done, and largely published, independently; but early in the 1930's, the publications of Speiser (1930; 1932a; 1933b) particularly encouraged ethnic and historical interpretations of the archaeological data. Woolley's excavation at Alalakh, Tell Atchana, west of the Euphrates in Syria from 1937 to the outbreak of the second World War, raised fresh questions and provided new evidence not assimilated into the debate until after the war when work was resumed between 1946 and 1949. This work is especially relevant to the present inquiry in the way it not only offers stratigraphic information on painted pottery styles of the earlier second millennium B.C. other than Khabur Ware, but also includes Nuzi Ware in context. It is these five key sites upon which the present inquiry is exclusively concentrated. Of these, Chagar Bazar yields the most extensive information on the development of Khabur Ware and is examined first, followed by Nuzi, where the continuous ceramic sequence from the late third to the late second millennium B.C. best illustrates the development of Nuzi Ware. The connection between these two categories of painted pottery can be seen at Tell Billa and Tell Brak, which together provide the earliest north Mesopotamian link to the ceramic sequence at Alalakh.

2.1. Chagar Bazar

Chagar Bazar (Pls. I-IV) is situated in the upper Khabur Valley on the Wadi Dara. The excavations conducted by Mallowan in the 1930's uncovered fifteen levels of occupation ranging from the fifth millennium to the mid-second millennium B.C. Of these, only the latest period of occupation, level 1, concerns the present study. It is distinguished from the preceding level 2 by the character of its remains, particularly by the new shapes and techniques exhibited in the pottery. The predominance of tall flat-based vases with monochrome painted decoration in level 1 contrasts with the predominance of small undecorated black and grey burnished vases with rounded bases in level 2.

2.1.1. Sequence

Level 1 was subdivided into five subphases of occupation which correspond to the changes observed in the building plans of area B.D. (Mallowan:1937, 94).[4] Mallowan proposed the term "Khabur Ware" to designate the painted pottery which first occurs in the earliest phase A of level 1 (Mallowan:1937, 102, Pl. I:1). The pottery in question

---

[4] These sub-phases are limited to a small area and do not necessarily apply to the mound as a whole. Moreover, the ceramic sequence obtained from these soundings could be affected by the nature of the building in which the pottery was found. In one phase, jars may be abundant because the area was a storage room, while in the next phase, cups and beakers may be predominant because the area in question has become a residential quarter. The change in ceramic typology may therefore reflect a functional change of the architectural context rather than a stylistic development. Unfortunately, the small scale of the excavation prohibits the identification of the buildings.

is wheelmade and consists mainly of large jars most probably intended for storage. These jars are made of coarse ware and the usual shape has a wide mouth, a high neck, and a flat or disk base, although another common variant has a more globular body and a shorter neck (Pl. I:6, 8-12; Pl. II:2-13). The decoration consists of painted monochrome designs which are sometimes combined with ribbing. The painted design is executed in matt red, reddish brown, or black, is usually confined to the neck, shoulder, and upper part of the body, and is strictly rectilinear. The basic element underlying the organization of every design is the horizontal band which either forms the entire decoration as a series of broad and narrow bands, or is combined with a frieze of simple geometric motifs. The repertoire of motifs is extremely limited, consisting mainly of triangles (hatched, cross-hatched, or concentric), sometimes with the addition of dots inside and outside. Other less frequent motifs include plain hatching, cross-hatching, zigzags, V's, and a running lozenge pattern.

The term "Khabur Ware" was extended to include other shapes found in level 1 which also had painted decoration of one sort or another. The carinated bowl with painted strokes on the rim is a distinctive type (Pl. I:7; Pl. II:1; Mallowan:1937, Fig. 22:2). Miniature versions of the larger jars and pots are included (Pl. I:10; Pl. III:4, 8, 10, 11, 13, 16, 17, 19, 20; Pl. IV:1 also Mallowan:1936, Fig. 22:7, 8 and Fig. 23:4) as are beakers (Pl. IV:6, 10 also Mallowan:1936, Fig. 14:13), and smaller more delicate types of vases (Pl. I:17; Pl. III:6, 12, 15, 18, 21; Pl. IV:2, 4). At first, Mallowan maintained that there was little perceptible change in the form or design of Khabur Ware throughout the five phases of level 1. Later, however, he noted that there was a tendency for the larger jars and pots made of coarse buff ware to occur in the earlier phases and for the smaller vases made of well-refined creamy clay to occur towards the end of the period (Mallowan:1937, 102). In terms of the five subphases of level 1, the large coarse jars occur to a limited extent in phase A, are abundant in phases B and C, decrease in number by phase D, and do not occur in the latest phase E. The smaller jars and more delicate vases continue to the latest phase E in which one sherd of Nuzi Ware was also found (Pl. IV:9). A closer look at the various types and their analogues will demonstrate that the large, flat-based jars with painted geometric design are perhaps not as unprecedented as is contended. Furthermore, some of the more delicate vases are distinct in shape, ware, and function from the rest of the Khabur Ware assemblage and most probably represent a different ceramic tradition.

2.1.2. Dates

Tablets assigned by Smith to the First Dynasty of Babylon were found in the ashy deposit at the very bottom of the lowest phase A and these provided a *terminus post quem* of c. 2000 B.C. for level 1 (Mallowan:1937, 94). Mallowan later amended this date to c. 1800 B.C. because of specific references in the text to Iasmah-Adad (son of Shamshi-Adad I c. 1815-1785) as governor of the city (Mallowan:1947, 82). The following phase B is dated tentatively between 1750-1700 B.C. on the basis of a "Syro-Hittite" cylinder seal (Mallowan:1937, Pl. XII: no. 1 and 3). The suggested dates for phases C and D are c. 1700-1650 B.C. and 1650-1550 B.C., respectively. The last phase E is dated to c. 1550 B.C. by one sherd of white-painted Nuzi Ware (Mallowan:1947, 83). In chronological terms, then, the large jars range between c. 1800 B.C. (or earlier) and c 1600 B.C., and the smaller types occur between 1750 B.C. and 1550 B.C. (or later).

2.1.3. Comments

The apparent discontinuity in the pottery sequence between levels 2 and 1 at Chagar Bazar was interpreted as evidence for the influx of new peoples bringing new ceramic types from outside northern Mesopotamia (Mallowan:1947, 22-23). However, the many parallels between the large, flat-based jars from Chagar Bazar level 1 and the jars from earlier periods at Brak, Billa, and Gawra suggest that the break in the sequence at Chagar Bazar may reflect a gap in time.[5] The flat base, for example, which does not occur at Chagar Bazar before level 1 can be found in Sargonid and Ur III period contexts at Brak (Pl. I:18-22), Tepe Gawra (Pl. I:24; Pl. II:14,15), and Tell Billa (Pl. I:23). One of the more common painted patterns on the larger jars from phases A-C of level 1 at Chagar Bazar is composed of horizontal lines separated by a row of hatched triangles with dots between the apices (Pl. I:1, 8, 10; Pl. II:3). At Gawra, an analogous design can be found on the large flat based jars of level VI. The decoration is likewise confined to the shoulder and consists of black painted dots interposed between incised triangles (Speiser:1935, 54). Similarly at Billa, in stratum 5, Speiser reports large jars decorated between the shoulder and the rim with a double rope moulding beneath a row of incised triangles filled with parallel strokes (compare Pl. II:4, 5, 7) and painted dots occasionally added in between (Speiser:1933a, 254). The same combination of incised hatched triangles and painted black dots recurs in the next stratum 4 at Billa (Speiser:1933a, 257) which corresponds in time to level 1 at Chagar Bazar.[6] The tree motif inserted between hatched triangles on a jar from Chagar Bazar (Pl. II:10) can be found in the earlier painted designs of Tepe Gawra stratum X (Pl. II:17-19) and is similar to the earlier incised decorations in the Diyala region (Pl. II:3). The foregoing comparisons suggest that the painted bands and hatched triangles on Khabur Ware from Chagar Bazar merely reflect a translation from a relief and incised form to a painted form of decoration. The ribbing seen on some of the jars at Chagar Bazar may be a vestige of earlier relief decorations (Pl. I:12, 16; Pl. IV:5 also Mallowan:1936, Fig. 16:2, 3).

Phases B and C include both the large jars with geometric designs and smaller miniature versions made of fine creamy clay and decorated exclusively with horizontal bands (Pl. III:4, 7, 8, 9, 10, 11, 14; Pl. IV:1 also Mallowan:1937, Fig. 22:7, 8 and Fig. 23:4; 1947, Pl. LXXXII:5). Also of finer ware and still more delicate constitution are cups with flaring rims, wide shoulders, and small disc or button bases (Pl. I:17; Pl. III:6, 12, 15, 18, 21; Pl. IV:2, 3, 4 also Mallowan:1936, Fig. 17:6, 7). These cups cannot be matched among the earlier larger shapes, but can be traced to undecorated prototypes in the Diyala region and in southern Mesopotamia where they are particularly common during the Larsa and old Babylonian periods (Compare Pl. I:17 with 25-26 and Pl. III:6 with 24-25). Most of these cups at Chagar Bazar are decorated with horizontal bands in the same manner as the miniature versions of the large coarse ware jars. Two exceptions have triangles drawn in a cursory fashion between bands which are reminiscent of the design on the larger coarse ware jars (Pl. III:12; Pl. IV:2). Other shapes included among the Khabur assemblage, but of southern origin, are beakers (Compare Pl. IV:6, 8, 10 with 11-12 and with Pl. V:21-22 and Pl. VII:15) and the carinated bowls (Pl. I:7; Pl. II:1). It is

---

[5]Kühne:1976, 10 compares the pottery from Chagar Bazar levels 2-5 with the metallic ware from Tell Chuera, dated to the Early Dynastic II-III period.
[6]The dating of Tell Billa is tentative, see below 2.3.2.

worth noting that the earliest evidence of south Mesopotamian types occurring in association with level 1 at Chagar Bazar is a wide shallow bowl made of smooth well-levigated clay which was found just below phase A and is, therefore, roughly contemporary with the earliest coarse ware jars (Mallowan:1947, 250 Pl. LXXXI:1). It is possible that the trend towards smaller and technically more refined vases at Chagar Bazar was, in part, influenced by the introduction of south Mesopotamian wares (and perhaps potters) beginning in phase A and increasing towards phases B and C.

In summary, the large jars made of coarse ware and decorated with horizontal bands and geometric motifs at Chagar Bazar have antecedents in the earlier flat-based jars with incised and relief decoration which occur at neighboring north Mesopotamian sites. This painted version first appears in phase A, dated c. 1800 B.C. or earlier, contunues to phase D, c. 1600 B.C., and overlaps with the finer miniature types in phase B and C. At this time (c. 1750-1700) the beakers and shoulder cups of south Mesopotamian origin are introduced. These have no coarse ware antecedents at Chagar Bazar, and are further distinguished from the local assemblage by the fact that they function as drinking rather than as storage vessels. They are decorated almost exclusively with horizontal bands, much like the miniatures mentioned above, and they continue in use into the 15th century B.C. when they overlap with Nuzi Ware.

2.2. Yorgan Tepe (Nuzi)

Yorgan Tepe (ancient Nuzi, Pls. V-VII) is located in the Zab basin, 13 kilometers southwest of Kirkuk. The site was excavated in the 1920's, and work was concentrated mainly in the uppermost levels in which several thousand cuneiform texts dating to the mid-second millennium B.C. were discovered. Textual references to "Nuzi" indicate the name by which the city was then known, and the great majority of Hurrian personal names suggest that the city population was predominantly Hurrian-speaking. Lower levels produced tablets of the Akkadian period which refer to the city as "Gasur" and the personal names do not reflect a significant Hurrian population. The ceramic sequence from the Gasur to the Nuzi periods was obtained from each of three separate excavation areas: Pit L4, Pit N120, and the temple site, and the results were relatively consistent. In each case, the Gasur levels were linked to the Nuzi levels by a transition period (Starr:1938, 26, 38-9, 62ff.).

2.2.1. Sequence

Most of the pottery discussed in the publication is derived from the temple site and is classified as "cultual terracotta" (Starr:1938, 367). Included among these, are several types which first occur in the Gasur period (Temple G) and persist through the transition period (Temple F) to the Nuzi period (Temples E-A). Dark grey burnished sherds with incised and white-filled designs were found below the level of Temple G, but are considered identical to the incised and white-filled Larsa Ware which is common in the Diyala and at Telloh (Compare Pl. V:1-5 with 6-8 and Genouillac:1936, Pl. D). The same technique of decoration is used to indicate the legs, feet, and feathers on a bird vessel from the transition period (Starr:1938, Pl. 59E), and in the Nuzi period, the incised and white-filled decoration is applied almost exclusively to burnished bowls

(Starr:1938, 402; Pl. VI:1-3). Zoomorphic vessels are attested in the Gasur level (Starr: 1938, Pl. 59, A, H) and are a common type of temple paraphernalia in the Nuzi period when they occur usually in the form of jars with added or incised features of a lion (Starr:1938:Pls. 103L-107A). The shoulder cup first appears in the Gasur period when it already exhibits the features which become distinctive of the later Nuzi types: a small foot, a bulbous lower body, a shoulder, and a high rim. The early examples have a hollow foot (Pl. V:9) which becomes solid by the end of the transition period (Pl. V:10, 11, 13). The shoulder cups of the Nuzi period retain the same basic features, but show considerable variation in shape (Pl. VI:4-14). The ware is characterized by its fine-grained texture and extreme thinness, and the regularity of the shape, surface, and thickness is attributed to highly skilled turning. Decoration is uncommon on these cups, but occurs occasionally in the form of white painted designs. The high cup is identical to the shoulder cup in ware and workmanship, and has a similar small foot and rounded lower body. However, instead of carinated sides it has straight sides and almost always has a decoration of white painted designs on a dark painted ground (Pl. VII:10-13). The combination of the high cup (or pedestal goblet) and white painted designs is most typical of Nuzi Ware, although the technique of decoration is also applied to shoulder cups as mentioned, and occasionally occurs on shapes and wares of other ceramic types (Pl. XII:15 also Starr:1938, Pls. 73L, 75N, 90N, and 132A). A similar process of refinement can be observed in the development of the plain, straight, or concave sided cup (beaker) which first appears in the transition period (Pl. V:14-16) and is characteristic of the Nuzi period. The early beakers have a plain flat base which first gradually diminishes in diameter (Pl. VII:2-3) and then acquires a flat foot (Pl. VII:4-5). As the size of the cup decreases, the foot becomes increasingly elaborate (Pl. VII:6-9).

One isolated example of Khabur Ware is published from Nuzi and is assigned to the transition period (Pl. V:12). It is a large storage jar made of coarse ware. The painted decoration is confined to the shoulder and neck and consists of a row of hatched triangles between horizontal bands. Starr identifies the abrupt shoulder and downward slope of the lip as typical Gasur features, and he compares the painted, hatched triangles to similar incised triangles on a storage jar of the same period (Starr:1938, 389-90, Pl. 58).

2.2.2. Date

The dating of the periods at Nuzi is aided by textual evidence. The tablets found in levels V, IV, and III of Pit L4 are written in old Akkadian and provide a Sargonid date for the latter part of the Gasur period. A tablet of the Ur III period found in or above the deposit III-IIB of Pit L4 and some Cappadocian tablets from level IIA of the same test pit suggest a tentative Ur III-Larsa date for the transition period (Eliot in Starr: 1938, 519). The beginning of the last phase of the Nuzi period is dated c. 1500/1475 B.C. by a letter from Šaušattar of Mitanni found in stratum II which corresponds to Temple A (Starr:1938, 122).

2.2.3. Comments

The ceramic sequence from Gasur to Nuzi has a direct bearing both on the problem of identifying the component types of Khabur Ware, and on the question of a transition between Khabur Ware and Nuzi Ware. The shoulder cup of the Gasur period at Nuzi is a cognate of south Mesopotamian types which originate in the Sargonid period and continue through to the Kassite period. One of these types is a cup with a remarkably tall neck, a squat bulbous body and a pedestal base (*UE* II, Pl. 255:74, *UE* VIII, Pl. 40:35), and another type which perhaps bears a closer resemblance to those at Nuzi is a vase with an everted rim, rounded shoulders and a small button base (*UE* II, Pl. 266:237, *UE* VII, Pl. 106: 58a and b, *UE* VIII, Pl. 46:89). The development of the shoulder cup at Nuzi is closely linked with that of its analogues in the south. This link is particularly evident during the Isin-Larsa and old Babylonian periods when the Diyala and south Mesopotamian examples provide numerous parallels to the types found at Nuzi. (Compare Pl. V:10-11 with 17-19 from the Diyala region; Pl. VI:4-8 with 15 from Ur; Pl. VI:9 with 16 from the Diyala region; Pl. VI:10, 12, 13 with Pl. III:24-25 from Nippur). It is interesting to note that many of the Isin-Larsa and old Babylonian types cited in the comparisons above are also found at other sites in northern Mesopotamia and northern Syria where they occur in contexts dated roughly to the 17th century B.C. and, are generally included among the later variety of Khabur Ware (Compare Pl. VI:6 and 8 with Pl. I:17 from Chagar Bazar; Pl. VI:9 with 17 from Assur and 19 from Brak; Pl. VI:12-13 with 18 from Assur, 20 and 21 from Billa, Pl. III:21 and Pl. IV:4 from Chagar Bazar, Pl. XII:10-11 from Jidle, and Pl. XV:7 from Alalakh) as are the two examples found at Kültepe in Anatolia (Pl. XV: 8-9). At Nuzi the shoulder cup is usually plain, while most, but by no means all of its analogues in northern Mesopotamia and Syria are decorated with painted horizontal bands. The Babylonian shoulder cups can always be differentiated from the local wares and shapes in these northern regions by virtue of their extremely fine texture and characteristic features: the high, sometimes everted rim, the sharply defined shoulders, and the small button or pedestal base. The plain, straight, or concave sided cup (beakers) also originates in the Sargonid period in southern Mesopotamia (Woolley:*UE* II, Pl. 251:10, 13, 14a) and continues to the old Babylonian period (Woolley:*UE* VII, Pl. 113:130). It is most common, however, in the Diyala region during the Isin-Larsa period which corresponds to the time when this type of cup is first introduced at Nuzi (transition period) (Compare Pl. V:15 with 20 from Tell Asmar; Pl. V:16 with 21 and 22 from Tell Asmar; Pl. VII:1 with 14 from Ishchali; Pl. VII:2 and 3 with 15 from Khafaje; Pl. VII:8 and 9 with 16 from Ur). Again, many of the Larsa period beaker shapes appear at various other sites in northern Mesopotamia and northern Syria, where some are decorated with dark painted designs and, like the shoulder cups, are included among the Khabur Ware assemblage (Compare Pl. V:16 and Pl. VII:3 with Pl. IX:13 from Billa and with both Pl. XI:1 and Pl. XIII:4 from Brak; Pl. VII:2 and Starr:1938, Pl. 76:C with Pl. IV:6 and 10 from Chagar Bazar, with both Pl. XIV:6 and Pl. XV:6 from Alalakh, and with Pl. XV:21 from Tepe Gawra; Pl. VII:6-7 with 17 from Alalakh). The high cup can likewise be traced to undecorated prototypes in the south where it is found in graves of the Ur III period and is a common form of deposit in the Larsa period (Compare Pl. VII:10, 11, 13 with Genouillac:1936, Pl. lll:1a and c – Ur III types not illustrated – and Pl. VII:21 from Telloh, and with 18 from Nippur; Pl. VII:12 with 19 from Ur and 20 from Tell Asmar). At Nuzi and at most of the other northern sites mentioned above, it appears towards the mid-second millennium B.C. and is generally associated with white painted designs. All three of the shapes discussed—the shoulder cup, the beaker, and the high cup (pedestal goblet)—are Babylonian shapes which are introduced to the north during the second millennium B.C. The fact that the shoulder cup, in particular, is quite often decorated with dark painted bands, does not necessarily link it to the northern Khabur Ware assemblage, for unlike the Khabur Ware shapes (as will be seen below) the shoulder cup has no local northern antecedents. Nor should the dark painted decoration of the shoulder cup divorce it entirely from the white painted goblets with which it shares not only a common origin and a very similar refined constitution, but also the same function as a drinking vessel. In short, the shoulder cup should not be included under the heading of 'Khabur Ware', but appears, instead, to be more closely connected with the development of Nuzi Ware.

The relation between the shoulder cup and high cup (pedestal goblet) is perhaps more apparent at Nuzi than at other sites. It has been mentioned that they are identical in ware and workmanship. Both are of the same origin, serve as drinking vessels, and are probably luxury wares. Decoration in both cases occurs for the first time in the mid-second millennium and is exclusively in the form of white painted designs on a dark painted ground. Clearly at Nuzi, the term 'Nuzi Ware' should include both the shoulder cup and the pedestal goblet and it merits a separate classification only with respect to its unique painted designs. The technique of white painting may itself have been derived from the grey-burnished incised and white-filled bowls which occur in the same period at Nuzi and which also appear to be of southern Mesopotamian origin. Woolley pointed out that white on dark paint produces the same effect as the incised and white-filled technique on a dark burnished surface (Woolley:1955, 349), and the two forms of decoration are further linked by the common use of certain designs: stippled triangles, zigzags between horizontal bands and diamond patterns. What then remains distinctive of Nuzi Ware is the combination of these local geometric patterns with foreign elements of design: aquatic bird, spirals, scrolls and palmettes.

2.3. Tell Billa

Tell Billa (Pls. VIII-IX) is situated 35 kilometers northeast of Mosul in the upper Tigris basin. During the two seasons of excavation under the direction of Speiser, work was confined to a relatively small area in the interest of obtaining a complete stratigraphic sequence down to virgin soil. The occupation of Billa begins with stratum 7, c. 3000 B.C., and its development runs parallel to that of the neighboring site of Tepe Gawra until the mid-second millennium B.C. when Tepe Gawra is abandoned. Billa continues to be occupied until the Late Assyrian period which is represented by level 1 (Speiser:1933a, 249-50). A brief review of the pottery from the earlier strata will give an indication of the local ceramic development leading up to the introduction of Khabur Ware and Nuzi Ware in strata 4 and 3.

2.3.1. Sequence

Stratum 7 is characterized by both coarse and finely levigated painted wares of which the chalice is the most typical type. The decoration is strictly monochrome and the design is frequently arranged in a triglyph-metope scheme between groups of horizontal bands which cover the entire body of the vase. The designs include both geometric and natural motifs: rows of triangles with the apex of one pointing towards the base of the next one, cross-hatching, saw-tooth patterns, stylized trees, checkerboards, and rows of birds drawn in silhouette (Speiser:1933a, 252). In stratum 6, the ceramic production is technically more advanced. The pottery is now made of finely levigated clay, is fired at higher temperatures, and is generally more elaborate in shape. Painted designs are nearly replaced by a new form of relief and incised decoration and the designs are exclusively geometric (Speiser: 1933a, 253). In the following stratum 5 there is an apparent decline in the variety of ceramic types. Large jars with flat or slightly curved bases are introduced with decoration limited to the region between the shoulder and the rim. Some of the more elaborate designs consist of rows of incised triangles filled with parallel strokes and placed over a double rope moulding (Pl. VIII:1). Occasionally dots of black paint are placed between the triangles. Some of the smaller vases are reported to have decorations of plain red bands (Speiser:1933a, 254). In stratum 4, there is a greater variety of shapes. Ornamentation, which had declined during the preceding period, is now again on the rise, particularly in the form of painted and incised designs. The pattern of incised triangles alternating with black dots is continued from stratum 5, as is the plain banded decoration. The latter occurs on a large jar which, however, only vaguely resembles the large coarse Khabur Ware jars decorated in a similar manner from Chagar Bazar (Compare Pl. VIII:6 with Pl. II:11). Another large jar from stratum 4 has a bistre and black design composed of bands, lattice and saw-tooth patterns, and hatched and concentric triangles (Pl. VIII:7). This particular jar has been identified as an example of Khabur Ware (Pl. VIII:13 from Chagar Bazar is compared to it). It should, however, be emphasized that although the decoration is entirely geometric, as is the case on the Khabur Ware jars from Chagar Bazar, it is bichrome and is composed of a more varied repertoire of motifs, many of which can be traced to earlier local painted wares in strata 7 and 6. Speiser himself notes that there is a superficial similarity in motifs and a practical identity of background between the wares of stratum 7 and stratum 4 (Speiser:1933a, 256). A much closer match to the Khabur assemblage at Chagar Bazar is the carinated bowl with parallel transverse strokes on the rim (Compare Pl. VIII:3-4: with 10-12 from Chagar Bazar), but this shape is considered Babylonian in origin (Mallowan:1937, 139). Naturalistic motifs occur on a small cup and on sherds found in stratum 4 (Pl. II:20 and Pl. IX:2 also Speiser:1933a, Pl. LXXII). These motifs are frequently arranged in combinations such as goats nibbling at trees, an animal or a tree between two mountains represented by triangles, and birds standing on quadrupeds. As Speiser noted, all of these combinations are paralleled on Palestinian bichrome ware (Speiser:1933a, 272). Stratum 3 is said to represent the first break in the cultural sequence. Both the principal shapes and the painted designs are introduced for the first time. Of the two most characteristic shapes, one is the cup, commonly known as a shoulder cup, which at Billa can be "u" shaped, "v" shaped or globular and is supported on a distinctive button base (Pl. IX:8, 9, 11). All variations of this cup are made of a fine fabric and are decorated almost exclusively with horizontal red bands applied to the upper part of the vessel. These cups correspond in shape, fabric, and decoration to the "younger" Khabur Ware shoulder cups at Assur (Pl. IX:21), and to the cups at Chagar Bazar (Pl. IX:19; Pl. III:6, 15, 18; Pl. IV:4). One cup of this type at Billa has an additional row of birds in silhouette above the horizontal bands (Pl. IX:10). The second characteristic shape is the slender pedestal goblet which is also made of a fine and thin fabric, but is decorated in the Nuzi style with white painted designs. In general, the designs are superimposed on three horizontal registers of black or red paint. Geometric patterns are predominant, but natural motifs are not uncommon and include birds, goats, and fish (Pl. IX:15-17).

2.3.2. Date

The date of stratum 4 was determined by stylistic comparisons and a few assumptions. The identity of the pictorial combinations on the sherds from Billa and those on the Palestinian bichrome ware provides a synchronism in the late 17th-early 16th century B.C., the approximate date for bichrome ware (Amiran:1970, 154). For reasons which are not quite clear[7], Speiser suggests that the Billa 4 ware originated in the north and that it first appeared at Billa before reaching the west coast in the late 17th century. On this premise he estimates the beginning of stratum 4 at c. 1900 B.C. (Speiser:1933a, 276). Stratum 3 at Billa is correlated with stratum II at Nuzi which also contained Nuzi Ware and is dated c. 1500 B.C. (see 2.2.2). Speiser believes that the Hurrians, who are held responsible for the introduction of Nuzi Ware (see 4.2) entered northern Mesopotamia from the west and, therefore, settled Billa several generations earlier than Nuzi. He consequently dates stratum 3 slightly earlier than Nuzi stratum II to the period 1600-1400 B.C. (Speiser:1933a, 274, 276).

2.3.3. Comments

The foregoing review of the ceramic development at Billa indicates that there is a general continuity in wares and decoration from the initial period of occupation up to stratum 3, which Speiser believes to be unique insofar as the main ceramic shapes and the decorative motifs appear for the first time (Speiser:1933a, 258). Painted and incised wares were developed in the earliest strata 7 and 6 and contain elements of design that can be followed through to the decoration on the pottery in strata 5 and 4. This is, no doubt, the reason why the large painted jars of stratum 4 (Pl. VIII:6 and 7) appear to be more closely affiliated to the earlier local ceramic wares than to the contemporary Khabur Ware from the upper Khabur valley, and it is, therefore, perhaps more apt that they be referred to as painted local wares.

The introduction of new shapes and designs in stratum 3 at Billa is not an isolated phenomenon.[8] The two principal shapes (shoulder cup and pedestal goblet) are paralleled at a number of sites in northern Mesopotamia and northern Syria (Assur, Gawra, Chagar Bazar, Jidle 3 and 2, and Alalakh V) where they are introduced at approximately the same time (late 17th-16th century) from southern Mesopotamia (see 2.2.3). It has been noted earlier in connection with Nuzi that the shoulder cup and pedestal goblet are related not only in their common origin, but also in their function and fabric. The association between the development of the two types is reinforced at Billa by the fact that both first appear in stratum 3. It should be emphasized that the shoulder cups and pedestal goblets of the Larsa and old Babylonian periods in southern Mesopotamia are undecorated and that the painted decoration seen on those at Billa in stratum 3 is strictly a north Mesopotamian feature. As southern shapes adopted and decorated by

---

[7]Speiser: 1933, 272-3. Speiser includes both Khabur Ware types and animal representations in his Billa 4 pottery. Despite noted parallels, he refutes the possibility that animal representations were derived from Palestine because the pottery shapes involved do not resemble those of bichrome ware. He suggests instead that the introduction of animal motifs was connected with the southward migration of the Hyksos from their presumed origin northeast of Billa.

[8]The same argument applies here as was presented above in n. 4.

north Mesopotamian ceramic schools, the shoulder cups and pedestal goblets of Billa 3 may be regarded as painted foreign wares.

The distinction between painted local wares and painted foreign wares is more apparent at Billa than at other sites in northern Mesopotamia because they are separated stratigraphically: the former occurs in stratum 4 and the latter, in stratum 3. This stratigraphic division is important in terms of differentiating the assemblage of Khabur Ware (and related types) from that of Nuzi Ware[9], but it should not, as it seems to have done, eclipse the definite continuity between strata 4 and 3. Not only do Babylonian ceramic types occur in stratum 4 as well as in 3 (Compare Pl. IX:1 with 5 from Ur and 6-7 from the Diyala region; Pl. IX:3 with 4 from Tell Asmar), but the tradition of painting and several of the decorative elements which occur in stratum 3 can be traced back to local wares of earlier periods. Plain banded decoration, for example, is reported on smaller vases from stratum 5, occurs on the large storage jar from stratum 4, and in stratum 3 it is characteristic of the shoulder cups and underlies the white painted designs of the pedestal goblets. Most indicative of the continuity between strata 4 and 3, however, is the continued use of naturalistic motifs in the decoration of pottery. Speiser describes the differences between the bird and animal representations on the Nuzi Ware goblets of stratum 3 and the naturalistic designs on the sherds of stratum 4 in terms of a development in technique and arrangement. The animals of stratum 4 are always drawn in silhouette and are generally arranged in antithetic groups. Those on Nuzi goblets of stratum 3 are drawn in outline with a filling of dots, strokes, or cross-hatching and are arranged in running friezes (Speiser:1933a, 259-260). However, the birds depicted on one shoulder cup from stratum 3 (Pl. IX:10) fall between Speiser's two groups as they are drawn in silhouette like those of stratum 4, but are arranged in a continuous frieze like those on the Nuzi goblets. The same is true of the dark painted birds on the censer from stratum 3 (Speiser:1933a, Pl. LXIII). It seems that the new white painted technique of stratum 3 does not displace the ongoing local tradition of dark painted geometric and naturalistic designs and that therefore its introduction, like that of the new Babylonian shapes, is not indicative of a cultural break, but merely represents a development in fashion and artistic style.

2.4. Tell Brak

Tell Brak (Pls. X-XII) is situated in the upper Khabur valley, to the southeast of Chagar Bazar and to the west of the river Jaghjagha and its tributary the Wadi Radd. In the course of three campaigns conducted between 1937-1938, six principal sites were investigated on the mound. It is interesting to note that the last quarter of the third millennium B.C. (Sargonid-Ur III periods) which is missing at Chagar Bazar, is represented at Tell Brak in three areas (sites C.H., E.R., F.S.). Second millennium material, however, was found only in one site, H.H., where four stratigraphic phases were determined on the basis of architectural remains.[10]

[9] See n. 4.
[10] See n. 4.

2.4.1. Sequence

The lowest level 4 contains Khabur Ware down to a depth of 7.3 meters below which appeared incised sherds followed by still lower deposits of black burnished ware. The level above 4, level 3, contained sherds of large shallow bowls decorated with broad bands of red paint. These are found in the upper two levels as well and correspond to similar examples found at Alalakh in level IV (Mallowan:1947, Pl. XLIII:5 and Woolley:1955, P. LXXXVIIIe). Cups with button bases first appear in this level 3 as do sherds of coarse pottery with designs of birds, quadrupeds and human figures in black paint on a buff ground (Pl. XI:2-8, also Mallowan:1947, Pl. LXXVIII). Mallowan compares some of the birds which are drawn in a distinctive style – with a round head and a dot for the eye, a tear shaped body, and a wedge shaped tail – to similarly depicted birds on Palestinian bichrome ware (Mallowan:1947, 239-40). The somewhat distorted quadrupeds and human figures on the bichrome and monochrome sherds from Alalakh VI and V are stylistically particularly close to those represented on the dark painted sherds at Brak (Compare Pl. XI:2-5 with 11 and 13 from Alalakh; Pl. XI:8 with 13 and 14 from Alalakh). The fact that these dark painted sherds at Brak are contemporary with the first few examples of white painted Nuzi Ware in level 3, is sometimes cited as evidence for a transitional phase between Khabur Ware and Nuzi Ware (Kantor in McEwan: 1958, 24). One solitary beaker, decorated with white reserved triangles in a red wash background and considered a late form of Khabur Ware, also coincides with the introduction of Nuzi Ware (Mallowan:1947, 225; (Pl. XI:1). The following level 2 is separated from level 3 by a deposit of ash, but the ceramic types continue unaffected. Dark on light decoration is still found in level 2 (Mallowan:1947, Pl. LXIV face vase; Pl. XII:1-4) although the white-on-dark Nuzi style is now predominant and is seen almost exclusively on the pedestal goblet with thin walls. The white design is confined to horizontal bands of dark paint and is usually arranged in a continuous frieze which is composed largely of geometric motifs: stippling, stippled circles, triangles, bands, zigzags, free and interlocking spirals, hatching, etc. (Pl. XII: 5-9). Level 2 ends in destruction which is followed by level 1 containing examples of Nuzi Ware, and both unpainted goblets (Pl. XIII:6-8), and shoulder cups (Pl. XIII:1-3).

2.4.2. Dates

The dates estimated for the upper three levels range between 1550 B.C. for the beginning of level 3 and c. 1350 B.C. for the end of level 1. The date for level 3 is based on that assigned to Nuzi Ware at Nuzi where it coincides with the reign of Šaušattar in the 15th century B.C. The destruction of level 2 is correlated with that of Alalakh IV which is now dated c. 1425-1400 B.C. (see 2.5.2), and level 1 is believed to have extended down to the 14th century B.C. because a number of glass fragments which were found in this level are associated with the Middle Assyrian period (Mallowan:1947, 78).

2.4.3. Comments

The Khabur Ware which is reported in level 4 is unfortunately neither described nor illustrated so that it is not possible to determine whether it belongs to the older large and coarse variety with geometric designs and/or to the more refined miniature variety with plain banded decoration. However, several of the Sargonid-Ur III pottery types which are described and illustrated do closely correspond in shape to the large Khabur Ware storage jars from Chagar Bazar (Pl. X:1-5). Mallowan observed that there is a considerable number of both tall functional jars with high necks and flat or ring bases and jars/pots of the squatter variety made during the Sargonid period. These are all wheel-made and are decorated frequently with ribbing and only rarely with incised and painted designs (Mallowan:1947, 219). Many of these jar and pot types are said to last through the Ur III period and, therefore, are likely antecedents of the large, coarse Khabur Ware jars which, at Chagar Bazar, could date back to the beginning of the second millennium B.C. (see 2.1.3).

As mentioned above, the overlap between dark painted designs and white painted designs in levels 3 and 2 is considered evidence of a transitional stage between Khabur Ware and Nuzi Ware. There are certainly elements which are interchangeable between the two techniques of painting. Several motifs and patterns which occur frequently in dark painted designs are reproduced in white painted designs (birds, checkerboard and rows of triangles pointing alternately up and down (Compare Pl. XI:2 and 4 with Pl. XII:1-2 and Mallowan: 1947, Pl. LXXVIII:4). Dark painted decoration occurs on shapes, including the pedestal goblet, which are otherwise decorated in the white painted technique (Pl. XII:1-4). One particular pedestal goblet has a painted pattern of broad and narrow horizontal bands which recalls the decoration of the small shoulder cups elsewhere (Compare Pl. XII:3 with Pl. XIII:11 from Assur, Pl. XIV:9 from Billa, and Pl. XV:12 from Assur). In another case, both techniques of decoration – dark painted and white painted – are combined on one sherd (Pl. XI:6). However, the theory of a transitional stage between Khabur Ware and Nuzi Ware is applicable only if one believes, as Mallowan and others do, that the dark painted sherds whose original shapes cannot be reconstructed, are examples of Khabur Ware because of their coarse ware and the dark paint. If, on the other hand, one argues that naturalistic motifs such as birds, quadrupeds, and human figures never occur on the large coarse Khabur Ware jars whose decoration is strictly geometric and that, therefore, these sherds, although also made of coarse ware, cannot be Khabur Ware, then a "transitional stage" is no longer applicable. At best, the occurrence of animal representations indicates an assimilation of new motifs into a local repertoire of design. In this respect, the evidence at Brak coincides with that at Billa. There is a remarkable parallelism between the early dark painted animal representations from both these sites and the bichrome representations in Palestine. Contact with the west is maintained through the following period when both shallow bowls with red bands and Nuzi Ware link Brak level 2 of site H.H. with Alalakh IV.

Brief reference to the soundings at Jidle in the Balikh valley (Mallowan:1946) is relevant at this point as its ceramic sequence complements that at Brak. The shoulder cup with plain banded decoration which is derived from undecorated prototypes in southern Mesopotamia and which appears in the north at Assur (Pl. IX:21), Billa 3 (Pl. IX:8, 9, 11), and Chagar Bazar (Pl. III:6) is also found at Jidle in level 3 (Pl. XII:10). In the following level 2, a similarly shaped cup is decorated with a stylized dark painted bird above a geometric pattern. The same combination of a dark painted bird above a very similar geometric pattern occurs on a pedestal goblet also from level 2 (Pl. XII:11-12), and both of these dark painted vases coincide with white painted Nuzi Ware. Thus, here as at Brak and Billa, dark painted designs overlap with white painted designs. At Jidle the shoulder cup and pedestal goblet are associated not only by the fact that both are contemporary and can be traced via painted analogues in northern Mesopotamia to undecorated prototypes in southern Mesopotamia, but also by the fact that both are decorated in the same dark painted technique with very similar designs. It is interesting to note that none of the large coarse variety of Khabur Ware is mentioned at Jidle, which could be attributed to a gap, proposed by Kühne (1976, 70), of over one millennium between levels 4 and 3; the latter is dated by its Nuzi Ware to the mid-second millennium B.C.

The following picture is obtained from the combined evidence of Billa, Brak and Jidle: undecorated Babylonian shapes filter into the north Mesopotamian ceramic assemblage between the 17th-16th centuries B.C. and from there continue with painted decoration to the region west of the Balikh river at a time (c. 16th century) which roughly corresponds to the introduction of western decorative elements and wares into north Mesopotamia.

2.5. Tell Atchana (Alalakh)

Alalakh, Tell Atchana (Pls. XIV-XV) lies in the Amuq plain east of the Orontes river. Woolley identified seventeen building levels on the basis of the succession of houses in the residential area and he assigned all of the remains to the Bronze Age (Woolley:1955, 5). Although only the pottery of levels VII-IV is of immediate concern, the painted pottery of the earlier levels has entered into discussions on Khabur Ware and therefore will be briefly reviewed here.

2.5.1. Sequence

Levels XVII-VIII are characterized by a fairly uniform repertoire of trefoil-mouthed jugs and carinated bowls. The decoration consists of a painted metopic arrangement which, in the case of the jugs, is filled with bird, animal, or geometric motifs. The jugs are further characterized by an "eye" motif at the side of the mouth, and the bowls have transverse strokes painted on the rim (Pl. XIV:1-4, also Woolley:1955, Pls. XC-XCII). In level VII, the Syrian painted pottery disappears and is replaced by a new range of shapes. Two shapes, in particular, are noteworthy because of their affinity to types common in Mesopotamia. One is a beaker (Pl. XIV:6) which is decorated with horizontal bands of red and black alternately on a buff ground (Woolley:1955, 314), and the other is a "beaker" with a slender foot (Pl. XIV:5). Level VII was destroyed by fire and the following two levels are poorly represented. The ceramic evidence for level VI is mostly derived from rubbish pits. Painted wares continued, but are now distinguished by a free style, and Palestinian bichrome ware is introduced for the first time. Mention has already been made of the similarities between the bird and animal designs of Alalakh VI, Brak level 3 in site H.H. and Billa stratum 4 (see 2.3.1 and 2.4.1). Also indicative of contact with the east is the increased number of beakers, several of which may have horizontal bands of paint (Woolley:1955, 327).[11] The material from level V is akin to that from level VI. Painted wares continue to show the same free style of decoration and, again, several comparisons can be drawn between individual bird and animal motifs at Alalakh and those further east at Brak (Compare the deer on Pl. XV:5 with that on Pl. XI:8) and Billa

---

[11] Woolley does not specify in which levels the beakers with banded decoration were found.

(Compare the birds on Pl. XIV:11, Pl. XI:11 and Woolley:1955, Pl. XCV:AT/46/269 with those on Pl. XIV:12-14). The shoulder cups with button bases and banded decoration which appear now at Alalakh for the first time (Pl. XV:7) are virtually identical to the shoulder cups at Billa in stratum 3 (Pl. XV:10-11), Assur (Pl. XV:12), and Chagar Bazar (Pl. III:6 and 15). The beaker shapes with flat bases (Type 94b - Pl. XIV:6) continue and new beakers with a foot are introduced (Type 93 - Pl. VII:17). Black-impressed ware occurs exclusively in level V (Pl. XV:1-4). It has a highly burnished surface which is decorated with incised or impressed geometric designs filled with a limestone paste (Woolley:1955, 342f.). Because neither the shape nor the design has a past history at Alalakh, Woolley concludes that black-impressed ware must have been an imported luxury item (Woolley:1955, 343). The same type of decoration was found at Tarsus where it is assigned to the Late Bronze I period c. 1650-1450 B.C. (Goldman:1956, Pl. 314, 315) and at Nuzi in stratum II (Pl. VI:1-3 and Starr:1938, 402 Pls. 91 and 92). The examples at both sites are technically identical to those of Alalakh but, according to Woolley, the differences in shape and elements of design preclude the possibility of direct influence linking the black-impressed wares from each of these three sites. Instead, Woolley postulates a fourth site somewhere in Anatolia as the common source for this ware at Tarsus, Alalakh, and Nuzi, and he attributes the differences in shape and design to separate local developments (Woolley:1955, 346-7). The pottery of the following level IV is distinguished by luxury wares of mainly Cypriote type. White painted designs first appear toward the end of the period. This form of decoration was applied to a wide range of shapes including the pedestal goblet (Type 118b - Pl. XV:15) which is typical of Nuzi Ware in northern Mesopotamia and both the flat based beaker (Woolley:1955, Type 94b - Pl. XIV:6) and the shoulder cup with a button base (Woolley:1955, Type 127 Pl. XV:7) which are also found decorated in the "Khabur" style with plain horizontal bands at Alalakh (Compare Pl. XV:13-14 with Pl. XII:3-4 from Brak and Pl. XII:12 from Jidle; Pl. XV:16-17 with 20 from Assur; Pl. XV:18 with Woolley:1955, Pl. LXXXVIIId and Pl. LXXXVIIa from Alalakh, Pl. XV:19 from Chagar Bazar, and 21 from Gawra).

2.5.2. Date

The chronology of the levels at Alalakh is adjusted according to the dates assigned to the archives found in levels VII and IV. A synchronism between Hammurabi of Yamkhad and Hammurabi of Babylon places the archive of level VII, which begins in the time of the former's son, Abbael of Yamkhad, after the destruction of Mari and the reign of Hammurabi of Babylon (Landsberger:1953, 52; Na'aman:1976, 129f.). The date of the level VII archive is, therefore, closely related to the dating of the First Dynasty of Babylon. The archive of level IV coincides with the Mitannian confederacy and its date depends on the dating of Šaušattar of Mitanni. The dating of both the First Dynasty of Babylon and Šaušattar of Mitanni is problematic. Roughly speaking, Alalakh VIII is assigned to the 19th century B.C. (Woolley:1955, 399). The beginning of level VII is c. 1720 B.C. while that of the VII archive is dated somewhat later (Collon:1975, 143-144; Na'aman, 1976:140), and it extends to c. 1650 B.C. or 1625 B.C. (Rowton:1962, 43 and Na'aman:1976, 140, respectively). Levels VI and V fall between the second half of the 17th century B.C. and the end of the 16th century B.C., the approximate beginning of level IV, which ends c. 1425-1400 B.C. (Woolley:1955, 399; Collon:1975, 167f.).

2.5.3. Comments

The Syrian pottery of Alalakh, the Amuq, and Cilicia is often compared with Khabur Ware (Hrouda:1957, 28) and has sometimes been regarded as its prototype (Perkins:1954, 50). Chronologically, this association appears to be feasible as the end of Syrian painted ware at Alalakh falls within the 19th century B.C. (level VIII) and may, therefore, coincide with the beginning of the large Khabur Ware storage jars in northern Mesopotamia (e.g. Chagar Bazar). Stylistically, however, there is little aside from individual motifs (cross-hatched triangles, double axes, X's) to support the theory of a direct lineage between the two wares. The characteristic trefoil-mouthed jugs and carinated bowls, the predominant triglyph-metope arrangement of the decoration, and the use of animal motifs all clearly distinguish the Syrian painted pottery from the Khabur Ware jars.

The Khabur Ware reported at Alalakh in level VII concerns one imported beaker with a bichrome decoration of alternating red and black bands which Woolley compares with an example from Brak (Woolley:1955, 314). There are no beakers with this type of bichrome decoration in northern Mesopotamia, and the shape alone does not warrant its identification as Khabur Ware. It has been indicated earlier that the beaker shape was introduced to northern Mesopotamia from Babylonia and this may also be the source of the isolated beaker in Alalakh VII (Compare Pl. XIV:6 and Pl. XV:6 with Pl. V:22 from Tell Asmar, with Pl. XIV:8 and 10 from Nuzi, and with *UE* VII:Pl. 113:130 = Old Babylonian). The "beaker" on a slender foot, which likewise appears in Alalakh VII for the first time, may also be traced to prototypes in southern Mesopotamia (Compare Pl. XIV:5 with 7 from Nippur).

In levels VI and V there are several indications of direct contact having been established between Alalakh and sites to the northeast. Not only do the bird and animal representations on bichrome ware at Alalakh bear some resemblance to those at Brak and Billa, but the shoulder cup with plain banded decoration known from Assur, Billa, Chagar Bazar and Jidle also appears at Alalakh in level V. In addition to these northeastern contacts, Alalakh seems to have maintained the older ties with southern Mesopotamia (originating in VII), at least through the period represented by level V, when the characteristic black-impressed ware, which Woolley traces to an unspecified Anatolian source, could conceivably have been introduced from southern Mesopotamia and the Diyala region where the same technique of design was current during the Larsa period (Genouillac, Telloh 11:1936, Pl. D; Diyala *OIP* LXIII, Pl. 123-125; Pl. V:6-7). A change in the foreign relations of Alalakh can be detected in the next level IV. The abrupt disappearance of black-impressed ware followed by the introduction of Nuzi Ware toward the end of the period suggests that the east-west contact between Alalakh and northern Mesopotamia were reinforced at the expense of the former north-south exchange between Alalakh and southern Mesopotamia.

Despite these and other developments in level IV (e.g. end of bichrome ware), there is a definite continuity between levels V and IV at Alalakh. As Woolley observed, many of the motifs which occur in the white painted designs of IV are also featured in the earlier white-filled impressed designs of V (Woolley:1955, 349). The link between these two techniques of decoration may be explained by the fact that the white painted style originated in northern Mesopotamia where it was contemporary with and was, no doubt, influenced by the Babylonian black-impressed ware (see 2.2.3). The continuity between V and IV is further indicated by certain ceramic shapes which are common to both levels, in particular the beaker and the shoulder cup with button base. While both of these shapes are generally associated with plain banded decoration (Alalakh VI-IV and northern Mesopotamia) they are also found with white painted Nuzi style decoration in level IV. Thus, at Alalakh white painted designs are applied to shapes otherwise associated with dark painted decoration. This fact complements the evidence at Jidle where dark painted designs are applied to the shape (pedestal goblet) otherwise associated with white painted decoration. Together, the evidence from Alalakh and Jidle reinforces the impression mentioned earlier that shoulder cups are directly linked to the development of Nuzi ware.

3. Definition of Khabur Ware and Nuzi Ware

3.1. Description

3.1.1. Khabur Ware

The preceding review of the painted pottery classified as Khabur Ware at several key sites in north Mesopotamia and north Syria has shown that Mallowan's term, which embraced the entire development of this pottery at Chagar Bazar from the large coarse ware shapes with geometric designs of the earlier phases to the smaller fine ware shapes with plain banded decoration of the later phases (Mallowan:1937, 102-3), cannot be maintained, nor can Hrouda's "older" and "younger" Khabur Ware, determined on the basis of the pottery from Assur which he found to run parallel to Mallowan's Khabur Ware sequence at Chagar Bazar (Hrouda:1957,22f.).

It is generally agreed that the "older" group of Khabur Ware is characterized by large thick-walled vessels made of coarse ware. The shapes may be broadly classified as receptacles but within this classification there is considerable variation from site to site. Storage jars, for example, occur with painted designs at Chagar Bazar, Tell Billa, Assur, Nuzi, Tell Taya, and Rimah but are more closely affiliated to their respective local ceramic assemblages than to each other. Khabur Ware is, therefore, less distinguished by its shape and ware than it is by its painted form of decoration which supplants earlier incised and relief decoration and has no immediate local antecedent. The painted decorations also vary regionally with respect to the arrangement and repertoire of motifs. At Chagar Bazar plain horizontal bands are prevalent. At Billa one painted jar has a bichrome design which is composed of a much more elaborate repertoire of motifs than is known elsewhere. The Khabur Ware at Assur is decorated mainly with geometric motifs which often occur in a triglyph-metope scheme. In concluding that painted decoration is the principal feature which distinguishes Khabur Ware from other indigenous wares, one should not overlook the numerous examples on which painting is combined with incised and relief designs (Chagar Bazar - Pl. I:12, 16, and Mallowan: 1936, Fig. 16:2-3, Tell Billa-Speiser:1933a, 254, 257: Tell Taya-J. Reade personal communication; Tell al Rimah-Oates:1970, 17, Pl. IX:2). Chronologically, these examples fall within the period of Khabur Ware and, stylistically, they may be considered transitional between the earlier incised and relief wares and Khabur Ware.

There is less of a consensus regarding the components of the "younger" group of Khabur Ware which, as yet, has not been defined satisfactorily. According to Hrouda, it is composed of small thin-walled vessels - primarily shoulder cups with button or nipple bases - which are made of a fine ware, have a smooth finish, and are decorated exclusively with horizontal bands (Hrouda:1957, 22, Tf. 8). [12] Mallowan would add the beakers and more refined miniature jars and pots which become prevalent in the later phases of level 1 at Chagar Bazar. As the term "younger" Khabur implicitly suggests that this group is descended from the "older" group of Khabur Ware, it should not include such shapes as the shoulder cup which is a Babylonian type and has no antecedents in the "older" Khabur Ware. Towards the middle of the second millennium it becomes increasingly difficult to isolate homogeneous ceramic groups. The term "younger" Khabur Ware, if used at all, should only apply to those smaller and possibly more refined vessels which have antecedents (both with respect to shape and decoration) in the "older" variety of Khabur Ware. The miniature jars and pots with plain banded decoration from the intermediate period of Chagar Bazar satisfy this description (Pl. III:2-4, 7, 8, 10, 11, 13, 14, 16, 17; Pl. IV:1, 5 see 2.1.1).

3.1.2. Nuzi Ware

Nuzi Ware has been distinguished primarily on the basis of its white painted decoration and secondly by its fairly standardized range of shapes: the pedestal goblet, the shoulder cup (cf. Nuzi, Brak and Alalakh), and the beaker (cf. Alalakh) are most common. It is significant that all of these characteristic shapes are also found decorated with plain red or black bands and, occasionally, with dark painted birds. These dark painted variants (Hrouda's "younger" Khabur Ware) should be regarded as a cognate of Nuzi Ware not only because the shapes are identical, but also because the organization of the decoration is virtually the same. In both cases, it is determined by horizontal bands arranged either in a series of registers, or in groups usually consisting of one wide band between two narrow ones. The white painted Nuzi Ware differs from the dark painted variety only with respect to its white painted design which is merely super-imposed on the horizontal bands.

3.2. Distribution

3.2.1. Khabur Ware

Attempts to establish the distribution of Khabur Ware are thwarted both by the absence of survey material from several pertinent areas and by the inadequacy of many reports on the material from those areas which have been surveyed. Only a few of the published surveys provide descriptions or illustrations of the Khabur Ware mentioned in the text, and when illustrations can be consulted, it often appears that the Khabur Ware mentioned refers to banded shoulder cups which, according to this study, should not be included among the Khabur Ware assemblage. [13] With this in mind, one might consider the most recent synthesis of the evidence

---

[12] Hrouda's "younger" Khabur group was formulated on the basis of the material from Assur which was largely derived from graves. These graves were rarely found intact (Haller:1954,3) and their contents are, therefore, of little chronological value and cannot be used to illustrate developments in the technique and style of ceramic production or decoration.

[13] For erroneous identifications of Khabur Ware see Kühne:1976.

for the distribution of Khabur Ware:

> ". . . Habur Ware occurs most densely within the northern Jazira. The area of its greatest distribution is bounded by the Euphrates on the west, the Zagros *chaine magistrale* on the east, the Hakkari, Tur Abdin, and Taurus chain south of Malatya on the north, and the arching line formed by the Jebels Hamrin, Sinjar, and Abd el Aziz on the south. There are isolated excavated occurrences beyond these borders (Kültepe, Mari, Nuzi, Dinkha)." (Hamlin:1971, 197).

While both the "older" and the "younger" variety of Khabur Ware (as defined here) occur at Dinkha Tepe, there are no banded shoulder cups. On the other hand, the illustrations of the material from Jidle 3 and Alalakh V reveal only banded shoulder cups, beakers and goblets and no examples of Khabur Ware. One might tentatively conclude on the basis of these observations that the distribution of Khabur Ware extends east of the Balikh river to the Ushnu-Solduz valley and differs from that of the banded drinking vessels which falls short of the Ushnu-Solduz valley but extends westward beyond the Balikh river to the Orontes valley.

3.2.2. Nuzi Ware

The distribution of white painted Nuzi Ware extends from the Zab valley east of the Tigris to the Amuq plain and Orontes valley in the west and as far south as Babylonia. [14] This area corresponds to that covered by the distribution of dark painted Nuzi Ware. Neither one occurs as far east as the Ushnu-Solduz valley or as far west as the Mediterranean coast.

3.3. Date

3.3.1. Khabur Ware

The approximate date for the beginning of the "older" Khabur Ware is provided by its association with cuneiform tablets in the lowest phase of level 1 at Chagar Bazar. The tablets were assigned to the First Dynasty of Babylon on epigraphic grounds, and Khabur Ware was dated to the reign of Shamshi-Adad I (c. 1817-1781 B.C.), a contemporary of Hammurabi of Babylon (c. 1792-1750 B.C.). Two examples of Khabur Ware are cited from Karum Ib at Kültepe. One is a miniature vessel with banded decoration which belongs to the newly defined "younger" Khabur Ware; the other is a shoulder cup also with banded decoration which corresponds to the early dark painted Nuzi Ware (Pl. XV:8 and 9). Both come from graves and are associated with tablets dated to *limu* officials of Shamshi Adad I (Balkan:1955, 43). If the absence of Khabur Ware from the earlier Karum II (dated by *limu* lists between Erisum I and Sargon I or Puzur Assur II (Garelli:1963, 78) is accepted as a *terminus post quem* for Khabur Ware, then its initial date could be pushed back from c. 1800 to c. 1900 B.C. which would in fact be corroborated at Chagar Bazar by an Ur III cylinder seal found in level 1 (Mallowan:1936, 29 and Pl. I:4). The lower date is determined at several sites (Billa, Gawra, Chagar Bazar) by a direct stratigraphic succession of Khabur Ware by Nuzi Ware. Thus the 16th-15th century date assigned to Nuzi Ware provides a *terminus ante quem* for Khabur Ware. The apparent

[14] For detailed discussion see Cecchini:1965.

lifespan of Khabur Ware in northern Mesopotamia is substantiated by radio carbon determinations for the Khabur Ware levels at Dinkha Tepe which, together with the dates for earlier and later material in the Hasanlu sequence, indicate a maximal range of c. 2000-1600 (Hamlin:1971, 303).

3.3.2. Nuzi Ware

The dark painted shoulder cups overlap with Khabur Ware in the intermediate period at Chagar Bazar and Kültepe in Karum Ib, and they appear in Alalakh V and Jidle 3 (c. 16th century B.C. see 2.5.1). The earliest attestation of banded shoulder cups occurs at Kültepe in Karum Ib (Pl. XV:9) and could date to the 19th century B.C., but, as Buchanan proposes on the basis of glyptic typology (Buchanan:1969,758), Karum Ib may have continued to the latter part of Hammurabi's reign (c. 1750 B.C.). In any case, these dark painted cups appear slightly earlier than the white painted goblets which are dated to the 15th century B.C. by their association with tablets of the time of Šaušattar, King of Mitanni at Nuzi str. II and Alalakh IV. If the white painted goblets represent, as has been suggested, a fully developed stage of Nuzi Ware, then possibly the initial stages of development are represented by the banded shoulder cup. The majority of painted shoulder cups are contemporary with white painted goblets and the lower date of Nuzi Ware is determined by the destruction of Nuzi stratum II which corresponds to the end of the Mitannian kingdom in the 14th century B.C.

3.4. Origin

3.4.1. Khabur Ware

Several fundamental assumptions have influenced previous attempts to determine the provenance of Khabur Ware. Both the conviction that Khabur Ware appeared suddenly on the north Mesopotamian scene and that it entirely displaced the older indigenous tradition of burnished wares led to the conclusion that Khabur Ware must have been introduced from outside. Its origin was thus sought in the neighboring traditions of painted pottery found to the east in Iran and to the west in Syria.

Speiser (1933a, 272-3), Mallowan (1937, 145 and 1947, 23f.), and Welker (1948, 191) traced Khabur Ware to northwestern Iran between the Azerbaijan and the Nehavend valley where they noted particularly close parallels in the painted pottery of Giyan II, then believed to be contemporary with Khabur Ware in north Mesopotamia. The comparisons include the horizontal arrangement of bands, the concentration of the design on the neck and shoulder of the vase, and such specific motifs as the double-axe, birds, and various forms of the triangle. It was argued that because the Giyan II material evolved from a long tradition of painted pottery which originated in Giyan IV, the origin of Khabur Ware could likewise be traced back to this earlier level at Giyan. The arguments against a Persian origin for Khabur Ware were in part conceded by the very proponents of this theory. It was observed that there is a greater range of painted shapes at Giyan, none of which approximate the large storage jars and carinated bowls typical of the "older" Khabur Ware in north Mesopotamia. It was further noted that at Giyan the repertoire of motifs is more varied, the designs are more complex, and the quality of painting is superior. More conclusive evidence against a Persian origin is provided by studies on the chronology of the late third and second millennium B.C. in north and central western Iran (Young:1965; 1966; 1969 and Dyson:1969) from which it appears that north Mesopotamian Khabur Ware predates at least part of the Giyan II painted assemblage and can not, therefore, be derived from it. A survey of the region showed, moreoever, that the Giyan II assemblage differed considerably not only from that of the preceding levels III and IV, but also from contemporary material of the surrounding sites, and that it most probably reflected a foreign element in Iran (Young:1969, 290). The painted pottery from Dinkha Tepe and Hasanlu VI is considered almost identical to Khabur Ware. (Pl. II:23; Pl. III:22-23, 26-28). Yet, neither one of these sites can be established convincingly as the source of Khabur Ware. According to radiocarbon dates, the relevant levels are contemporary with, but not earlier than the corresponding period of Khabur Ware in north Mesopotamia. In view of the fact that Dinkha Tepe and Hasanlu are situated outside the main area of Khabur Ware distribution and that close parallels with Khabur Ware are not attested further east beyond the Ushnu-Solduz valley (Hamlin:1971, 196, 301), it seems rather more likely that the presence of Khabur Ware at Dinkha Tepe and Hasanlu represents a temporary eastward extension of north Mesopotamian culture.

Perkins (1954, 50) and later Porada (1965, 172) suggested that Khabur Ware was derived from the painted pottery of northwestern Syria. Central to this theory is the evidence that Syrian painted pottery predates Khabur Ware. The sequence could be established at Kültepe where Syrian painted pottery was found in Karum levels IV and II (Özgüç: 1950, Pl. LXXIX, 617 and 616, respectively), while Khabur Ware first appeared in Karum level 1b. Similar evidence was cited at Alalakh where Syrian painted pottery occurs between levels XVII and VIII, but has fallen out of use by level VII, then thought to correspond roughly to the introduction of Khabur Ware in north Mesopotamia. As mentioned earlier (see 2.5.3), the differences in the shapes and the composition of design between Khabur Ware and Syrian painted pottery far outweigh the few parallels between individual elements of design which alone do not support a western origin for Khabur Ware. Beyond the realm of stylistic comparisons is the fact that Syrian painted jugs and carinated bowls have not hitherto been found east of the Euphrates (personal communication from J. Tubb), nor have Khabur Ware jars with geometric designs been attested west of the Balikh river (see 3.2.1). This discrepancy between the distribution of the two painted wares in question is perhaps the most compelling argument against deriving one from the other or, as suggested by Hrouda and Deshayes (see 1.), both from a third common source. Instead, it appears that Syrian painted pottery and Khabur Ware belong to entirely separate cultural spheres.

The numerous parallels between Khabur Ware shapes and designs and those of the local Sargonid and Ur III period point unequivocally to the conclusion that Khabur Ware was an indigenous north Mesopotamian development and that this development, to judge by the combination of painted, incised, and relief decoration on certain vessels, was neither as sudden, nor as radical as originally claimed.

3.4.2. Nuzi Ware

The shoulder cups and goblets of Nuzi Ware have been recognized as distinctly Mesopotamian shapes which can be traced to undecorated prototypes of the Ur III and Isin-Larsa periods in Babylonia. Although painted decoration is attested in the south, it occurs on other shapes and is of an entirely different character (e.g. Nippur-McCown and Haines: 1967, Pl. 88:18-23) than that which occurs later on the cups and goblets in the north where the underlying and often exclusive element of design is the horizontal band, a feature of Khabur Ware. The technique of a white on black design has been derived from a number of sources ranging from black-impressed ware (Woolley:1955, 349) to the mural paintings of Mari (Mallowan:1947, 241), and the alternating black and white patterns which occur on dark painted sherds from Brak level 3 (Hrouda:1957, 18-19; Kantor in McEwan: 1958, 23) all of which are Mesopotamian. The source of inspiration for the subject matter of these designs is, however, not confined to Mesopotamia. Comparisons of individual elements extend to Aegean pottery (Starr:1938, 397, Cecchini:1965, 46-47). Palestinian bichrome ware (Mallowan:1947, 240), Egyptian frescoes of the 12th Dynasty (Mallowan:1939, 894 n. 2), Halaf ware (Mallowan:1947, 238), the mural paintings at Mari and Nuzi (Mallowan:1947, 241-2), and Kirkuk style cylinder seals (Cecchini:1965, 46). As there are no two examples of Nuzi Ware with exactly the same white painted design, nor are there two sites where the Nuzi Ware decoration is conceived in exactly the same way (Hrouda:1957, 13-16), it is probable that not one but several diverse influences contributed directly or indirectly to the Nuzi style of decoration.

4.   Conclusions and Evaluation

4.1. Conclusions

Khabur Ware can be linked to the north Mesopotamian ceramic traditions of the Sargonid and Ur III periods on the basis of its similar shapes, coarse ware, and geometric designs. It is distinguished from these earlier wares only on the basis of its painted form of decoration, and it should, therefore, be regarded as an indigenous north Mesopotamian product which merely represents the last stage in a transition from incised and relief designs to painted designs. The lack of uniformity among the shapes and painted designs of Khabur Ware from different sites argues against attributing this ware to a single ethnic group or ceramic school. The diversity suggests instead that painted decoration was a fashion adopted separately by various village workshops and implemented according to local tastes. The actual technique of painting could have been acquired from a number of possible sources. One cannot, on the one hand, ignore the existence of the already established traditions of the late third to early second millennium B.C. painted pottery in the regions bordering on north Mesopotamia to the north in the Keban, the east in northwest Iran, and the west in northwest Syria. All three of these different painted wares overlap chronologically with the appearance of Khabur Ware in north Mesopotamia, and the technique of painting could have been transmitted by one or any combination of several conventional and unconventional means such as commercial and political contacts, travelling artisans, or semi-nomadic tribal groups who knew no political boundaries (Hamlin:1971, 280). On the other hand, one should not overlook the fact that north Mesopotamia has its own history of painted pottery, in particular the painted and incised Ninevite V ware belonging to the late fourth to early third millennium B.C. (Tepe Gawra VIIIA-VII, Tell Billa 7-6, Chagar Bazar 4-5, Tell Brak 5), and the "Early or Eggshell Khabur Ware" of the Early Dynastic period (Pl. II:21-22) known from Harran (Prag:1970, 79), Carchemish (Woolley:1921, Pl. 27.c.4), Amarna and Hammam (Woolley:1914, Pl.

XXII), Jidle 5 and 4 (Mallowan:1946, Fig. 10-11), and Mari (Parrot:1956, Fig. 107 nos. 1548, 1549). The latter is not comparable to Khabur Ware in either fabric or craftsmanship (Kühne:1976, 70), but if Khabur Ware designs are reminiscent of earlier local wares, as comparisons have shown (see 2.3.1 for Speiser's comparison between the Ninevite pottery of Billa stratum 7 and the Khabur Ware of stratum 4), then perhaps the revival of painting itself could also have been inspired by the rediscovery of earlier painted sherds. The "older" Khabur Ware storage jar, with its coarse fabric and basic rectilinear design, is uniquely prosaic. In this respect, at least, Khabur Ware is unparalleled in any of the three neighboring styles of painted pottery mentioned above, and this distinction rather speaks in favor of a local origin for the technique of painting as well as for the design.

Nuzi Ware incorporates elements from a number of earlier ceramic traditions. The shapes are fairly standardized and are characterized by delicate drinking cups and goblets derived from Babylonian prototypes. The designs defy classification. They can be either dark painted (usually on shoulder cups and beakers) but are generally white painted (usually on goblets). The subject matter includes geometric and naturalistic (animal and vegetal) motifs and reflects both Mesopotamian and foreign influence. The parallels for Nuzi Ware designs mentioned above (3.4.2) cover a broad chronological and geographical range as well as several different genres of decoration. The parallels extend from the sixth millennium B.C. to the mid-second millennium B.C. They reach from Egypt and the Aegean to Mesopotamia and they include frescoes and mural paintings, pottery and cylinder seals. Despite certain similarities, such as vegetal motifs and a basic geometric repertoire, the overall composition of Nuzi Ware decoration varies from site to site. Yet, the general statement can be made that in the west at Alalakh, the emphasis of design is on floral motifs, while further to the northeast at Brak, Assur, Billa and Nuzi, to mention but a few, the emphasis is on geometric patterns. The former has been attributed to Aegean influence, and the latter is most probably derived from the rectilinear designs of the north Mesopotamian Khabur Ware. The different spheres of influence reflected in the variable Nuzi Ware designs contrast with the fairly standardized shapes; a contrast which would be expected if the Nuzi Ware shapes were exported from a center of production to a number of sites where they were subsequently decorated by local artisans, perhaps upon commission.

The date and distribution of Khabur Ware and Nuzi Ware are two points of particular importance for which the evidence, however, is inadequate. There appears to be a significant difference between the distribution of Khabur Ware and Nuzi Ware which could be a function of change in the political and economic conditions. Aside from the isolated jar at Nuzi and the miniature vase at Kültepe, Khabur Ware is represented within an area defined by the Ushnu-Solduz valley to the east, the Zab river to the south, and the Balikh river to the west, and its distribution is seen as matching that of the Assyrian realm and its closest commercial contacts (Hamlin:1971, 295). Nuzi Ware supersedes Khabur Ware at many sites in north Mesopotamia, but its distribution differs from that of this earlier painted ware in that it is not represented beyond the Zab river east of the Tigris, while it is attested both to the south of the Zab river at Nuzi and later at Aqar Quf in Babylonia (Baqir:1945, Fig. 26), and to the west of the Balikh river in the Amuq plain. The distribution of Nuzi Ware is believed to correspond to that of the Mitannian confederacy (O'Callaghan:1948, 72). The approximate time when the shift from the political and commercial sphere of the Assyrian kingdom to that of the Mitannian kingdom occurred can be ascertained by following the distribution of the early undecorated

Babylonian shoulder cup and goblet which later characterize Nuzi Ware. The frequency of these two shapes at Nuzi in level F and in the Diyala region in the Isin-Larsa levels, and their occurrence at Alalakh in levels VII and VI suggest that early in the second millennium B.C., when Khabur Ware was produced in Assyria, the regions south of the Zab river and west of the Balikh river lay within the Babylonian sphere of commercial and cultural contact. [15] This material evidence for the extension of Babylonian influence is reinforced both by the Old Babylonian tablets from Larsa and Sippar which refer to trade between Larsa and Eshnunna in the Diyala region (Leemans:1960, 73f., 89-90), and by the Mari texts which attest trade in timber, wine, myrtle, and sweet reed from the north and northwest (Carchemish and Yamkhad) to Sippar and thence to the region east of the Tigris (Leemans:1960, 103). There is little mention of trade between Assur and the south (Ibid:98), yet the texts do indicate that there was rivalry between the kingdoms of Assur and Eshnunna over the possession of the land east of the middle Tigris — namely, Arrapha and Nuzi, and this may explain the presence at Nuzi of both north Mesopotamian Khabur Ware and south Mesopotamian shoulder cups and goblets.

The date for the introduction and decoration of shoulder cups and goblets in Assyria may be estimated by indirect evidence at Dinkha Tepe and Alalakh. As neither shoulder cups nor goblets occur at Dinkha Tepe, the lower (radiocarbon) date for Khabur Ware provides a *terminus post quem* of c. 1600 B.C., and the appearance of banded shoulder cups in Alalakh V provides a *terminus ante quem* of the mid-16th century B.C. Sometime, then, between 1600 B.C. and 1550 B.C. contact between Assyria and the Ushnu-Solduz valley was interrupted, and a three-way exchange was established between Babylonia, Assyria, and northern Syria (see 2.5.3). This marks the beginning of an international period which is later witnessed at its peak in the correspondence of the Amarna period when the extensive exchange of gifts and the many treaties sealed by dynastic marriages reinforced the contact between the 18th Dynasty in Egypt and the kingdoms of the Hittites, Mitannians and Kassites. This unprecedented level of cultural exchange is manifested in the eclectic style of the white painted designs on Nuzi Ware.

4.2. Evaluation

The foregoing study has a direct bearing on the question of a Hurrian material culture. "Hurrian" originated as a linguistic term to designate a language attested textually, largely in the form of personal names belonging to neither the Semitic nor the Indo-European language groups. The term acquired an ethnic connotation in reference to the people who spoke the language, and gradually it acquired a cultural meaning in reference to the archaeological material supposedly distinctive of the people who spoke the language. Thus, Nuzi Ware was considered an example of Hurrian material culture because it seemed to occur for the first time in association with texts containing a vast number of Hurrian names taken to reflect a predominant Hurrian population (Nuzi stratum II, and Alalakh level IV, cf. Speiser:1933a, 274). The association of Nuzi Ware with the Hurrians

---

[15] Babylonian cultural influence is also evident at this time in the pottery shapes encountered further east in Susa levels AXIV and AIX. (Compare Pl. VI:4 with *MDP* 47, Pl. 23 no. 3, 13; Pl. VI:6 with *MDP* 47, Pl. 23, no. 4; Pl. VI:12 with *MDP* 47, Pl. 21, no. 13, 15.)

was refuted on the grounds that the white painted pottery appeared long after the Hurrians
were attested in Assyria, and that it is not found at many sites where the existence of a significant Hurrian population has been inferred from textual references (e.g. Ras Shamra, Schaeffer:
1938, 35; Smith: 1938, 428). The present study contributes further to this line of reasoning:
the shapes of Nuzi Ware are not new to the 15th century B.C., but have a long history which
extends back to the Ur III period at Nuzi and in Babylonia, when Hurrian names occur only
sporadically (Gelb: 1944, 59). The white painted designs indicate a wide range of influence and
cannot, as a whole, be attributed to a single ethnic group. The Hurrians have further been linked
to the earlier introduction and distribution of animal representations and even painted decoration
from central Anatolia to Syria, northern Mesopotamia and Palestine following their textually
attested appearance in the Near East in the third quarter of the third millennium B.C. It has
been shown here, however, that Khabur Ware is an indigenous north Mesopotamian product
characterized by its diversity, which precludes also its equation with any single ethnic group.

As the painted pottery of the second millennium B.C. in northern Mesopotamia cannot convincingly be accredited to the Hurrians, its appearance and wide distribution have been explained
alternatively by developments in political and economic conditions (see 4.1). It has been
noted that the appearance of Khabur Ware coincided with the Assyrian colony period during
which Assyria attempted to secure control over the trade in valuable raw materials from inner
Iran to Cappadocia by establishing relationships with the tribal rulers of northwest Iran
and the Zagros foothills (e.g. Šušara - Tell Shimshara Laessøe: 1963, 146) and by conduct-
ing campaigns in the Khabur basin (Oates: 1968b, 39; Kupper: 1957, 212) and the upper
Balikh valley (e.g. Zalmaqum, Kupper: 1963, 8), thereby covering an area which corresponds
roughly to the distribution of Khabur Ware (Hamlin: 1971, 306 and Kramer: 1977, 96f.).
Similarly, the appearance and distribution of the initial stages of Nuzi Ware (dark painted
shoulder cups and goblets) coincided with the earliest indications of a confederation of
states under the Mitannian kingdom (the earliest mention of Mitanni occurs on the seal
of Šutarna son of Kirta at Alalakh and on an Egyptian inscription dated to Thutmosis I -
Na'aman: 1974, 267-8) which exerted political control across northern Mesopotamia and
Syria from the Zagros in the east to the Amuq and possibly Cilicia in the west and which
thrived as an intermediary in the trade between Babylon and the Syrian coast (see 4.1).
Implicit in this association of painted pottery with the rise of a political power dependent
upon the maintenance and effective exploitation of a stable and prosperous trading net-
work is the assumption that painted pottery is a luxury commodity which is largely
contingent upon court patronage. Nuzi Ware is regarded as a "luxury ware" (Mallowan:
1939, 893) or "Palace ware" (Mallowan: 1947, 243), and Khabur Ware is considered to
be a "court ware" (Hamlin: 1971, 295; Kramer: 1977, 98). In the case of Nuzi Ware, which
is defined by a fairly uniform repertoire of delicate drinking cups decorated with varying,
yet distinctive, white painted designs and found to a large extent in temples, palaces, and
residence of wealthy merchant families (Alalakh - Woolley: 1955, 119; Nuzi - Starr: 1938
Vol. II, 17-18; Tell 'Abyad - Baqir: 1945, 11, Pl. XXIV), this classification seems to be
applicable. However, it hardly seems pertinent in the case of Khabur Ware which includes
a great variety of mainly large and coarse ware storage vessels decorated with basic, and
often cursorily executed, dark painted geometric patterns and which is found, to a large
extent, in yet unidentified architectural contexts. In purely practical terms, Nuzi Ware,
though fragile, could be exported and decorated locally, which accounts for the homogeneity in its shapes and fabric contrasted with the diversity in the style and content of its

designs. Khabur Ware, on the other hand, was not transportable, which accounts for the lack of homogeneity from site to site both with regard to its shapes and designs.

Of the two types of painted pottery of the second millennium B.C. in northern Mesopotamia, Nuzi Ware qualifies as the more useful ceramic category which could serve as an indicator not of ethnic movements, but of political, economic and even social developments. Future studies may reveal more precisely the nature of the relationship between this luxury ware, with unique and individual designs, and its patrons.

Bibliography

el-Amin, M. and Mallowan, M.E.L.
  1950   "Soundings in the Makhmur Plain" *Sumer* 6,55-90.
Amiran, R.
  1961   "The Pottery of the Middle Bronze I in Palestine". *IEJ* 10:204-225.
  1970   *Ancient Pottery of the Holy Land.* New Brunswick.
Andrae, W.
  1938   *Das wiedererstandene Assur.* Leipzig.
Balkan, K.
  1955   *Observations on the Chronological Problems of the Karum Kaniš.* Türk Tarih Kurumu
          Yayinlarindan VII seri, No. 28, Ankara.
Baqir, T.
  1945   "Iraq Government Excavations at "Aqar Quf" - Second Interim Report, 1943-44".
          Iraq suppl.
Barrelet, M., ed.
  1977   *Methodologie et Critiques I. Problèmes concernant les Hurrites.* Centre de Recherches
          Archéologiques, Paris.
Braidwood, R.J.
  1937   *Mounds in the Plain of Antioch.* Chicago.
Buchanan, B.
  1969   "The End of the Assyrian Colonies in Anatolia: The Evidence of Seals". *JAOS* 89,758-762.
Burney, C.
  1970   "Excavations at Haftavan, 1968: First Preliminary Report". *Iran* 8,157-172.
Burton Brown, T.
  1951   *Excavations in Azerbaijan, 1948.* London.
Carter, E.
  1979   "Elamite Pottery, ca. 2000-1000 B.C." *JNES* 38, 111-128.
Carter, T.H.
  1965   "Excavations at Tell al-Rimah, 1964. Preliminary Report". *BASOR* 178,40-69.
Cecchini, S.M.
  1965   *La Ceramica di Nuzi.* Studi Semitici 15, Rome.
Charpin, D.
  1977   "L'onomastique hurrite à Dilbat et ses implications historiques". *Methodologie et
          Critiques I,* ed. Barrelet, 51-70.
Chéhab, M.
  1940   "Tombes phéniciennes: Majdalouna". *Bulletin du Musée de Be·· ·uth 4.*

Conteneau, G. and Ghirshman, R.
   1935   *Fouilles du Tepe-Giyan.* Musée du Louvre-Départment des Antiquites Orientales. Série Archéologique, Tome III, Paris.

Delougaz, P.
   1952   *Pottery from the Diyala Region. OIP* LXIII.

Deshayes, J.
   1959   (untitled) review of Hrouda 1957. *Syria* 36, 121-124.

Durand, J-M.
   1977   "L'insertion des Hurrites dans l'histoire Proche-Orientale: Problematique et perspectives". *Methodologie et Critiques* I, ed. Barrelet, 21-40.

Dyson, R.A., Jr.
   1969   "A Decade in Iran. *Expedition* 2, 39-47.

Emre, K.
   1963   "The Pottery of the Assyrian Colony Period According to the Building Levels of the Kaniš Karum." *Anatolia* 7, 87-99.

Engberg, R.M.
   1942   "Tombs of the Early Second Millennium from Baghuz on the Middle Euphrates". *BASOR* 87, 17-23.

Fugmann, E.
   1958   *Hama: Fouilles et recherches de la fondation Carlsberg 1931-1938. L'Architecture des périodes préhellenistiques.* Nationalmuseets Skrifter, Storre Beretninger IV. II, I, Kobenhavn.

Gadd, C.J.
   1940   "Tablets from Chagar Bazar and Tell Brak, 1937-1939." *Iraq* 7, 22-66.

Garelli, P.
   1963   *Les Assyriens en Cappadoce.* Bibliothèque archéologique et historique de l'institut français d'archéologique d'Istanbul XIX, Paris.

Garstang, J.
   1953   *Prehistoric Mersin.* Oxford.

Gasche, H.
   1973   *Ville Royale de Suse 1. La Potterie élamite du deuxième millénaire a. C.* Mission de Susiane, Mémoires, Tome XLVII.

Gelb, I.J.
   1944   *Hurrians and Subarians.* Studies in Ancient Oriental Civilization No. 22, Chicago.

Genouillac, H. de
   1936   *Fouilles de Telloh,* Tome II: Époque d'Ur IIIe Dynastie et de Larsa. Paris.

Goetze, A.
   1957a   "Alalakh and Hittite Chronology." *BASOR* 146, 20-26.
   1957b   "On the Chronology of the Second Millennium." *JCS* 11, 53-61 -61

Goldman, H.
   1956   *Excavations at Gözlü Kule, Tarsus,* Vol. I. Princeton.

Haas, V.
   1978   "Substratgottheiten des westhurrischen Pantheons". *Rev. Hittite* 36, 59-69.

Haller, A.
   1954   *Die Gräber und Grüfte von Assur. WVDOG* 65.

Hamlin, C.
   1971   "The Habur Ware Ceramic Assemblage of Northern Mesopotamia: An Analysis of Its Distribution." Unpublished Ph.D dissertation. University of Pennsylvania.
   1974   "The Early Second Millennium Ceramic Assemblage of Dinkha Tepe." *Iran* 12, 125-153.

Hansen, D.P.
   1965   "The Relative Chronology of Mesopotamia". Part II. *Chronologies in Old World Archaeology,* ed. Ehrich, R.W. Chicago.

Hayes, W.C., Rowton, M.B. and Stubbings, F.H.
  1962   "Chronology. Egypt; Western Asia; Aegean Bronze Age." *CAH* Fascicle 4.
Hrouda, B.
  1957   "Die bemalte Keramik des zweiten Jahrtausends in Nordmesopotamien und Nordsyrien".
          Istanbuler Forschungen 19.
  1958a   "Die Churriter als Problem archäologischer Forschung". *Archaeologia Geographica* 7, 14-19.
  1958b   "Waššukanni, Urkiš, Šubat-Enlil". *Mitteilungen der Deutschen Orient-Gesellschaft* 90, 22-35.
  1961   "Tell Fechērīje. Die Keramik". *Zeitschrift für Assyriologie Neue Folge 20, 201-239.*
Ingholt, H.
  1940   *Rapport préliminaire sur sept campagnes de fouilles à Hama en Syrie.* Kobenhavn.
Kenyon, K.
  1969   "The Middle and Late Bronze Age Strata at Megiddo". *Levant* 1, 25-60.
Kramer, C.
  1977   "Pots and Peoples". *Mountains and Lowlands,* Bibliotheca Mesopotamica 7, 91-112.
Kühne, H.
  1976   *Die Keramik von Tell Chuera und Ihre Beziehungen zu Funden aus Syrien-Palästina, der
          Türkei, und dem Iraq.* Berlin.
Kupper, J-R.
  1957   *Les nomades en Mésopotamie au temps des rois de Mari.* Paris.
  1963   "Northern Mesopotamia and Syria". *CAH*, Fascicle 14.
Landsberger, B.
  1954   "Assyrische Königsliste und dunkles Zeitalter". *JCS* 8, 1-73.
Laessφe, Jr.
  1963   *Peoples of Ancient Syria.* London.
Leemans, W.F.
  1960   *Foreign Trade in the Old Babylonian Period - as Revealed by Texts from Southern
          Mesopotamia.* Leiden.
Lloyd, S.
  1938   "Some Ancient Sites in the Sinjar District". *Iraq* 5, 123-142.
Mahmoud, Y.
  1970   "Tell al-Fakhar. Report on the First Season's Excavations". *Sumer* 26, 109-126.
Mallowan, M.E.L.
  1936   "The Excavations at Tall Chagar Bazar and an Archaeological Survey of the Ḥabur ·
          Region, 1934-5". *Iraq* 3, 1-86.
  1937   "The Excavations at Tall Chagar Bazar and an Archaeological Survey of the Ḥabur
          Region, Second Campaign, 1936". *Iraq* 4, 91-177.
  1939   "White Subartu Pottery". *Mélanges Syriens offerts à M. René Dussaud.* vol. III. Paris.
  1946   "Excavations in the Baliḥ Valley, 1938". *Iraq* 8, 111-159.
  1947   "Excavations at Brak and Chagar Bazar." *Iraq* 9, 1-259.
  1965   "The Mechanics of Ancient Trade in Western Asia". *Iran* 3, 1-7.
Mazar, B.
  1968   "The Middle Bronze Age in Palestine". *IEJ* 18, 65-97.
McCown, D.E., Haines, R.C., and Hansen, D.P.
  1967   *Nippur I. OIP* LXXVIII.
McEwan, C.W.
  1958   "Soundings at Tell Fakhariyah". *OIP* LXXIX.
Mellink, M.J.
  1972-5 Hurrian Art in *Reallexikon der Assyriologie,* vol. 4, 514-519.
Moortgat, A.
  1956   "Vorläufiger Bericht über eine Grabung auf dem Tell Fechērīje, 1955". *AAAS* VI, 39-50.
  1957   "Archäologische Forschungen der Max Frhr. von Oppenheim - Stiftung im nördlichen
          Mesopotamien". *AAAS* VII, 17-30.

1960   *Tell Chuera in Nordost-Syrien.* Wiesbaden.
1962   *Tell Chuera in Nordost-Syrien.* Köln ·
1975   *Tell Chuera in Nordost-Syrien.* Berlin.
1976   *Tell Chuera in Nordost-Syrien.* Berlin.

Munn-Rankin, J.M.
1956   "Diplomacy in Western Asia in the Early Second Millennium B.C." *Iraq* 17, 68-110.

Na'aman, N.
1974   "Syria at the Transition from the Old Babylonian Period to the Middle Babylonian Period".
        Ugarit-Forschungen Bd. 6, 165-274.
1976   "A New Look at the Chronology of Alalakh Level VII". *Anatolian Studies* 26, 129-143.

Oates, D.
1965   "The Excavations at Tell al Rimah, 1964." *Iraq* 27, 62-80.
1966   "The Excavations at Tell al Rimah, 1965". *Iraq* 28, 122-139.
1967   "The Excavations at Tell al Rimah, 1966". *Iraq* 29, 70-96.
1968a   "The Excavations at Tell al Rimah, 1967". *Iraq* 30, 115-138.
1968b   *Studies in the Ancient History of Northern Iraq.* London.
1970   "The Excavations at Tell al Rimah, 1968". *Iraq* 32, 1-26.

O'Callaghan, R.T.
1948   *Aram Naharaim.* Analecta Orientalia 26, Rome.

Orlin, L.L.
1970   *Assyrian Colonies in Cappadocia.* The Hague.

Özgüç, T.
1950   *Ausgrabungen in Kültepe, 1948.* Türk Tarih Kurumu Yayinlarindan V. seri, No. 10, Ankara.
1953   "Vorläufiger Bericht über die Grabungen von 1950 in Kültepe Ausgeführt in Auftrage des
        Türk Tarih Kurumu." *Belleten* 17, 109-118.

Paraayre, D.
1977   "L'Attribution de sculptures aux Hurrites: critique methodologique." *Methodologie et
        Critiques* I, ed. Barrelet,115-208.

Parrot, A.
1956   *Mission archéologique de Mari I, le temple d'Ishtar.* Paris.

Perkins, A.L.
1954   "The Relative Chronology of Mesopotamia". *Relative Chronologies in Old World Archaeology*,
        ed. Ehrich. Chicago, 42-55.

Porada, E.
1965   "The Relative Chronology of Mesopotamia, Part I." *Chronologies in Old World Archaeology*,
        ed. Ehrich. Chicago, 133-200.

Prag, K.
1970   "The 1959 Deep Sounding at Harran in Turkey." *Levant* 2, 63-94.

Reade, J.
1968   "Tell Taya (1967): Summary Report." *Iraq* 30, 234-264.

Sasson, J.M.
1966   "A Sketch of North Syrian Economic Relations in the Middle Bronze Age." *JESHO* 9, 161-181.

Schaeffer, C.F.A.
1938   "De quelques problèmes que soulèvent les découvertes de Tell Atchana." *Syria* 19, 30-37.
1948   *Stratigraphie Comparée et Chronologie de l'Asie Occidentale.* London.

Seton-Williams, M.V.
1953   "A Painted Pottery of the Second Millennium from Southern Turkey and Northern Syria."
        Iraq 15, 56-58.

Smith, S.
1938   "The City Nuzu". *Antiquity* 12, 425-431.
1940   *Alalakh and Chronology.* London.

al-Soof, B.
   1970   "Mounds in the Rania Plain and Excavations at Tell Basimusian (1956)". *Sumer* 26, 65-104.
Speiser, E.A.
   1930   *Mesopotamian Origins - The Basic Population of the Near East.* Philadelphia and London,
           120f.
   1932a   "The Bearing of the Excavations at Tell Billa and at Tepe Gawra upon the Ethnic Problems
           of Ancient Mesopotamia". *AJA* 36, 29-35.
   1932b   "The 'Chalice' Ware of Northern Mesopotamia and Its Historical Significance". *BASOR*
           48, 5-l0.
   1933a   "The Pottery of Tell Billa". *The Museum Journal* 23, 249-283.
   1933b   "Ethnic Movements in the Near East in the Second Millennium B.C. *ASOR*, Offprint series
           No. 1, 13f.
   1935   *Excavations at Tepe Gawra,* I. Philadelphia.
   1953   "The Hurrian Participation in the Civilization of Mesopotamia, Syria, and Palestine."
           Journal of World History No. 2 vol. 1, 311-327.
Starr, R.F.S.
   1938   *Nuzi.* Cambridge.
Swift, G.F., Jr.
   1958   The Pottery of the 'Amuq Phases K to O and its Historical Relationships. Unpublished
           Ph.D. dissertation, University of Chicago.
Thureau-Dangin, F. and Dunand, M.
   1936   *Til Barsib.* Paris.
Tobler, A.J.
   1950   *Excavations at Tepe Gawra,* II. Philadelphia.
Welker, M.
   1948   "The Painted Pottery of the Near East in the Second Millennium B.C. and its Chronological
           Background." *Transactions* of the American Philosophical Society vol. 38, Part 2, 185-265.
Woolley, Sir C.L.
   1914   "Hittite Burial Customs." *LAAA* VI, 87-98.
   1921   *Carchemish,* Part II. London.
   1955   *Alalakh.* Oxford.
Young, T.C., Jr.
   1965   "A Comparative Ceramic Chronology for Western Iran, 1500-500 B.C." *Iran* 3, 53-85.
   1966   "Survey of Western Iran, 1961." *JNES* 25, 228-239.
   1969   "The Chronology of the Late Third and Second Millennium in Central Western Iran as Seen
           from Godin Tepe." *AJA* 73, 287-291.

Plate I

Phase A
1. Mallowan:1937,Fig. 21:1 (3:20)*
2. Mallowan:1947, Pl. LXXXII: 13 (3:10)
3. Mallowan:1947, Pl. LXXXII, 16 (3:10)

Comparisons
4. *OIP* LXIII, Pl. 165. B.706.370 Larsa Period? (3:10)
5. *OIP* LXIII, Pl. 165, B.706.360 Larsa Period (3:10)

Phase B
6. Mallowan:1937, Fig. 21:4 (3:20)
7. Mallowan:1937, Fig. 16;8 (3:10)
8. Mallowan:1937, Fig. 21:12 (3:20)
9. Mallowan:1937, Fig. 23:11 (3:10)
10. Mallowan:1937, Fig. 23:7 (3:10)
11. Mallowan:1937, Fig. 23:10 (3:10)
12. Mallowan:1937, Fig. 22:14 (3:20)
13. Mallowan:1937, Fig. 22:9 (3:20)
14. Mallowan:1937, Fig. 24:10 (3:10)
15. Mallowan:1937, Fig. 24:9 (3:10)
16. Mallowan:1937, Fig. 24:6 (3:10)
17. Mallowan:1947, Pl. LXXXII, 8 (3:10)

Comparisons
18. Mallowan:1947, Pl. LXV:1 Tell Brak, Sargonid-Ur III Period (3:20)
19. Mallowan:1947, Pl. LXV:4 Tell Brak, Sargonid-Ur III Period (3:20)
20. Mallowan:1947, Pl. LXV:8 Tell Brak, Sargonid-Ur III Period (3:20)
21. Mallowan:1947, Pl. LXV:15 Tell Brak, Sargonid-Ur III Period (3:20)
22. Mallowan:1947, Pl. LXV:13 Tell Brak, Sargonid-Ur III Period (3:20)
23. Speiser:1933a, Pl. LV:4 Tell Billa, stratum 5 (3:40)
24. Speiser:1935, Pl. LXXI:161 Tepe Gawra, stratum V (3:20)
25. *UE* VII, Pl. 108:76 Ur, Old Babylonian (3:10)
26. *UE* VII, Pl. 108:77 Ur, Old Babylonian (3:10)

*Numbers in parenthesis refer to scale.

Pl. I

Chagar Bazar

Comparisons

Phase A

Phase B

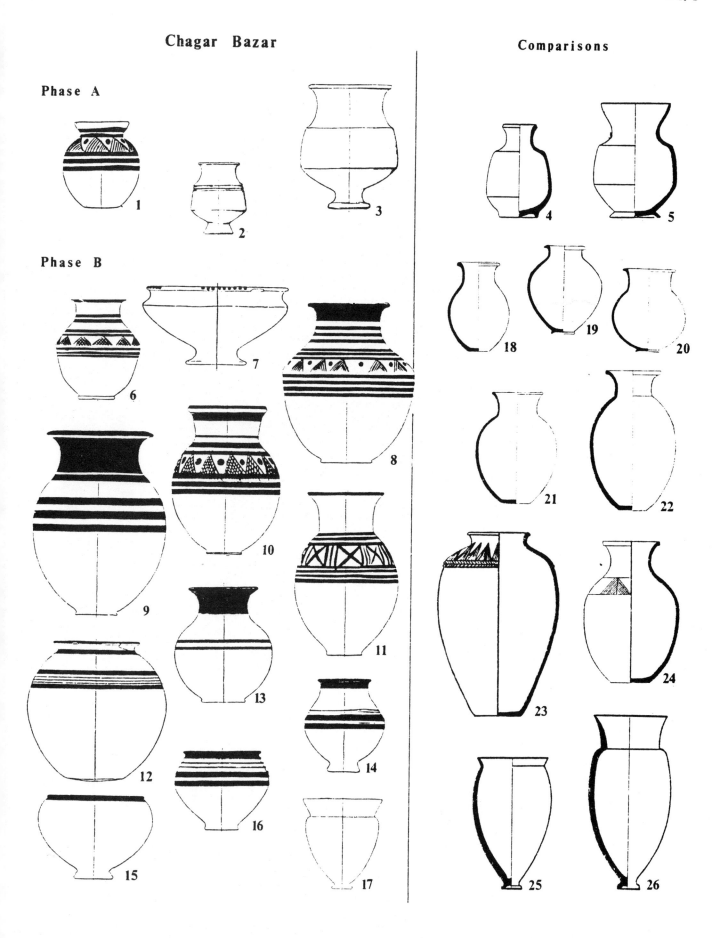

Plate II

Phase C
1.   Mallowan:1937, Fig. 23:1   (3:10)
2.   Mallowan:1947, Pl. LXXXII, 15   (3:10)
3.   Mallowan:1937, Fig. 21:11   (3:20)
4.   Mallowan:1937, Fig. 21:9   (3:20)
5.   Mallowan:1937, Fig. 23:5   (3:10)
6.   Mallowan:1937, Fig. 23:6   (3:10)
7.   Mallowan:1937, Fig. 21:10   (3:20)
8.   Mallowan:1937, Fig. 23:12   (3:10)
9.   Mallowan:1937, Fig. 23:13   (3:10)
10. Mallowan:1937, Fig. 21:8   (3:20)
11. Mallowan:1937, Fig. 16:13   (3:20)
12. Mallowan:1937, Fig. 23:8   (3:10)
13. Mallowan:1937, Fig. 16:15   (3:10)

Comparisons
14. Speiser:1935, Pl. LXIX, 134 Tepe Gawra, stratum VI?   (3:20)
15. Speiser:1935, Pl. LXIX, 135 Tepe Gawra, stratum VI   (3:10)
16. *OIP* LXIII, Pl. 193, D. 526.371 Diyala, ED III?   (1:10)
17. Tobler:1950, Pl. CLII, 525 Tepe Gawra, stratum X   (1:5)
18. Tobler:1950, Pl. CXLV, 398 Tepe Gawra, stratum X   (1:5)
19. Tobler:1950, Pl. CLII, 523 Tepe Gawra, stratum X   (1:5)
20. Speiser:1933a, Pl. LXXII Tell Billa, stratum 4
21. Parrot:1956, Fig. 107, 1548 Mari, niveau d (57:100)
22. Woolley:1914, Pl. 22, 1 Hammam   *
23. Hamlin:1974, Fig. XII, c Dinkha Tepe, strata 1-2   (1:4)

*72% of Kühne:1976:Abb. D, no. 5

Pl. II

Chagar Bazar

Comparisons

Phase C

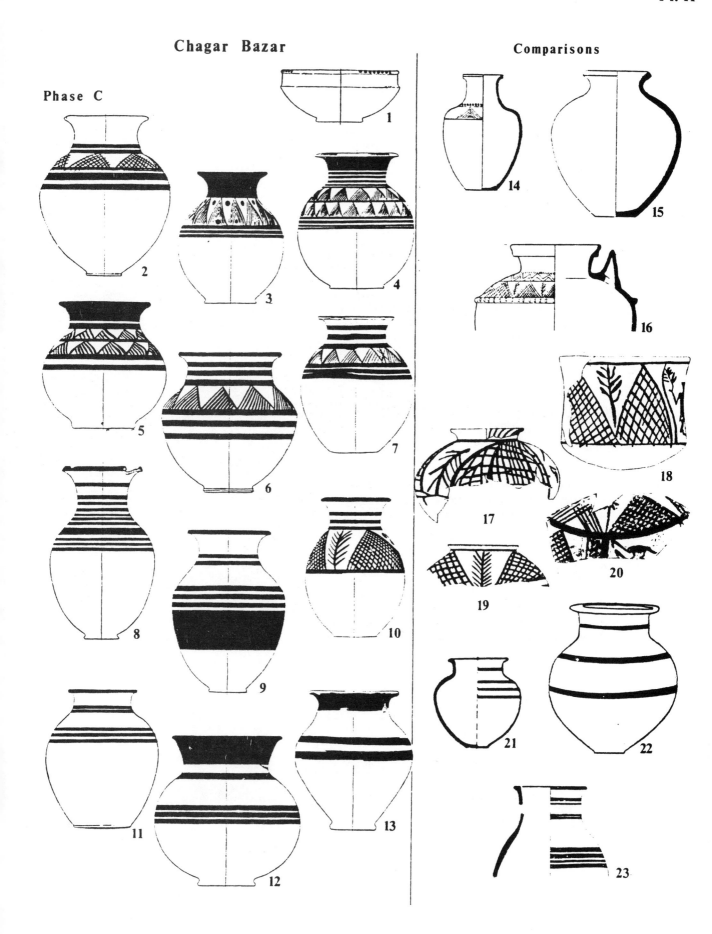

Plate III

Phase C

1. Mallowan:1937, Fig. 21:5   (3:20)
2. Mallowan:1937, Fig. 21:2   (3:20)
3. Mallowan:1937, Fig. 21:3   (3:20)
4. Mallowan:1937, Fig. 24:1   (3:10)
5. Mallowan:1937, Fig. 22:13   (3:20)
6. Mallowan:1947, Pl. LXXXII:17   (3:10)
7. Mallowan:1947, Pl. LXXXII:7   (3:10)
8. Mallowan:1937, Fig. 23:2   (3:10)
9. Mallowan:1937, Fig. 22:6   (3:20)
10. Mallowan:1937, Fig. 22:4   (3:20)
11. Mallowan:1937, Fig. 22:5   (3:20)
12. Mallowan:1937, Fig. 24:13   (3:10)
13. Mallowan:1937, Fig. 24:7   (3:10)
14. Mallowan:1937, Fig. 23:3   (3:10)
15. Mallowan:1947, Pl. LXXXII:6   (3:10)
16. Mallowan:1936, Fig. 17:3   (3:10)
17. Mallowan:1937, Fig. 24:8   (3:10)
18. Mallowan:1936, Fig. 17:5   (3:10)
19. Mallowan:1936, Fig. 17:2   (3:10)
20. Mallowan:1936, Fig. 17:1   (3:10)
21. Mallowan:1936, Fig. 17:4   (3:10)

Comparisons

22. Hamlin:1974, Fig. XII:e Dinkha Tepe, stratum 9   (1:4)
23. Hamlin:1974, Fig. XII:b Dinkha Tepe, stratum 4a   (1:4)
24. *OIP* LXXVIII, Pl. 94:5 (Type 35) Nippur, Old Babylonian   (3:10)
25. *OIP* LXXVIII, Pl. 94:8 (Type 35) Nippur, Old Babylonian   (3:10)
26. Hamlin:1974, Fig. I:2 Dinkha Tepe, stratum 3   (1:5)
27. Hamlin:1974, Fig. I:3a Dinkha Tepe, stratum 3   (1:5)
28. Hamlin:1974, Fig. I:3b Dinkha Tepe, stratum 8   (1:5)
29. Starr:1938, Pl. 78:I Nuzi, stratum II   (3:10)
30. Starr:1938, Pl. 78:F Nuzi, stratum II   (3:10)
31. Starr:1938, Pl. 78:E Nuzi, stratum II   (3:10)
32. Starr:1938, Pl. 78:G Nuzi, stratum III   (3:10)

Pl. III

Chagar Bazar

Comparisons

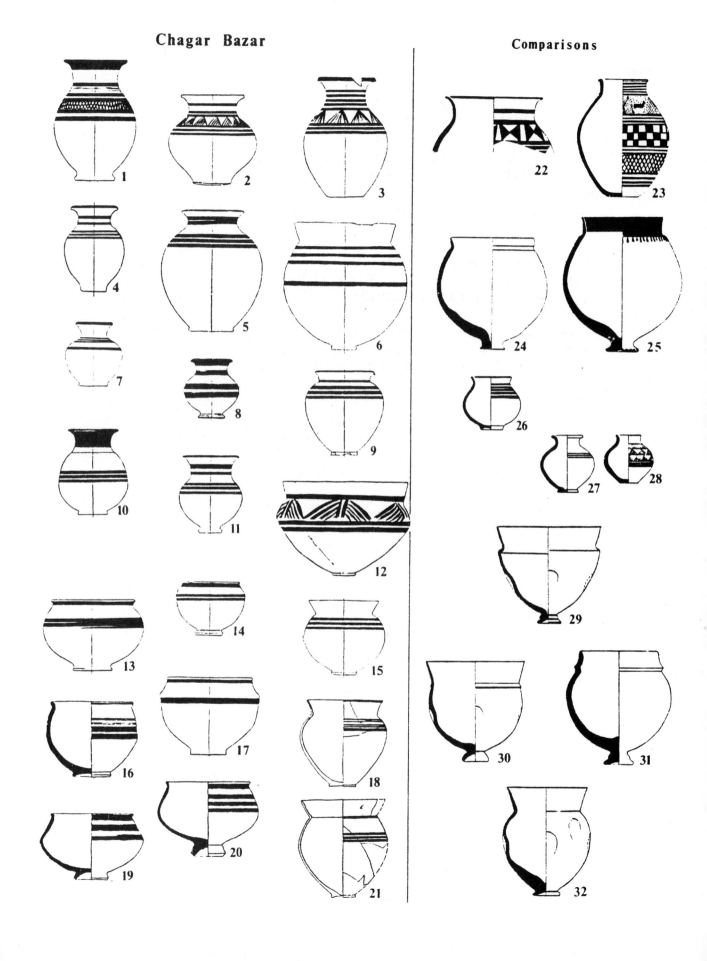

Plate IV

Phase D
1. Mallowan:1937, Fig. 24:2 (3:10)
2. Mallowan:1937, Fig. 24:14 (3:10)
3. Mallowan:1937, Fig. 24:4 (3:10)
4. Mallowan:1937, Fig. 24:11 (3:10)
5. Mallowan:1937, Fig. 22:11 (3:20)
6. Mallowan:1947, Pl. LXXXI:7 (3:10)

Comparisons
7. *OIP* LXIII, Pl. 161:B. 576.720a Khafaje, Old Babylonian (3:10)

Phase E
8. Mallowan:1937, Fig. 22:3 (3:20)
9. Mallowan:1936, Fig. 27:20 (Nuzi Ware) (3:10)
10. Mallowan:1947, Pl. LXXXI:6 (3:10)

Comparisons
11. Starr:1938, Pl. 76:K Nuzi, stratum II (3:10)
12. Starr:1938, Pl. 76:C Nuzi, stratum II (3:10)
13. Hamlin:1974, Fig. I:12 Dinkha Tepe, surface (1:5)

Pl. IV

Chagar Bazar

Comparisons

Phase D

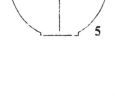
1

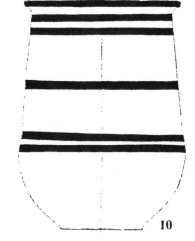
2

3

4

5

6

7

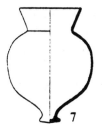

11

12

13

Phase E

8

9

10

11

Plate V

Gasur (Temple G)
1. Starr:1938, Pl. 56:J (3:10)
2. Starr:1938, Pl. 56:L (3:10)
3. Starr:1938, Pl. 56:P (3:10)
4. Starr:1938, Pl. 56:O (3:10)
5. Starr:1938, Pl. 56:S (3:10)

Comparisons
6. *OIP* LXIII, Pl. 123:k Tell Asmar, Larsa Period (3:5)
7. *OIP* LXIII, Pl. 123:h Tell Asmar, Larsa Period (3:5)
8. *OIP* LXXVIII, Pl. 92:12 Nippur, TB level IV 1, Ur III - Isin/Larsa (3:10)

Transitional (Temple F)
9. Starr:1938, Pl. 62:K (3:10)
10. Starr:1938, Pl. 78:C (3:10)
11. Starr:1938, Pl. 78:B (3:10)
12. Starr:1938, Pl. 70:B (1:12)
13. Starr:1938, Pl. 78:G (3:10)
14. Starr:1938, Pl. 62:T (3:10)
15. Starr:1938, Pl. 62:S (3:10)
16. Starr:1938, Pl. 63:A (3:10)

Comparisons
17. *OIP* LXIII, Pl. 160:B.556.720 Khafaje, Old Babylonian (3:10)
18. *OIP* LXIII, Pl. 161:B.576.720b Khafaje, Old Babylonian (3:10)
19. *OIP* LXIII, Pl. 161:B.576.720a Khafaje, Old Babylonian (3:10)
20. *OIP* LXIII, Pl. 153:B.236.200a Tell Asmar, Late Larsa (3:10)
21. *OIP* LXIII, Pl. 153:B.236.300 Tell Asmar, Late Larsa (3:10)
22. *OIP* LXIII, Pl. 153:B.237.100 Tell Asmar, Late Larsa (3:10)

Pl. V

Yorgan Tepe (Nuzi)

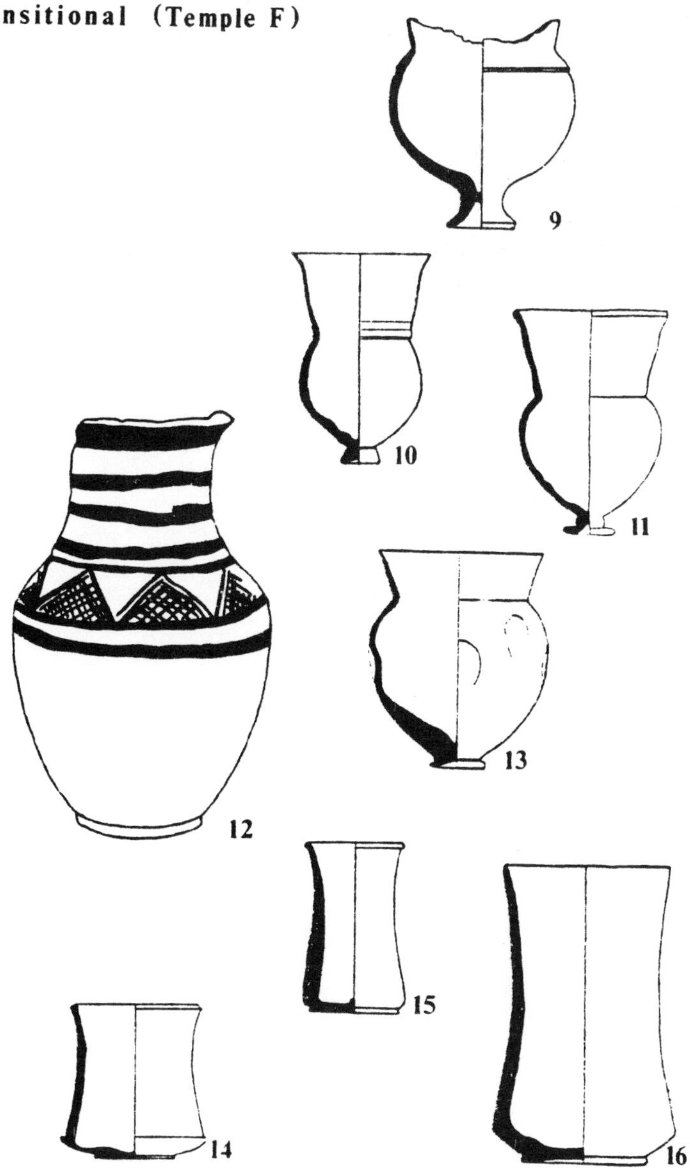

Comparisons

Gasur (Temple G)

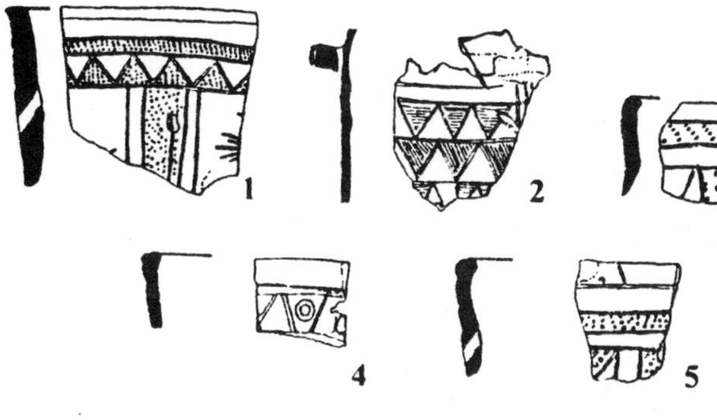

Transitional (Temple F)

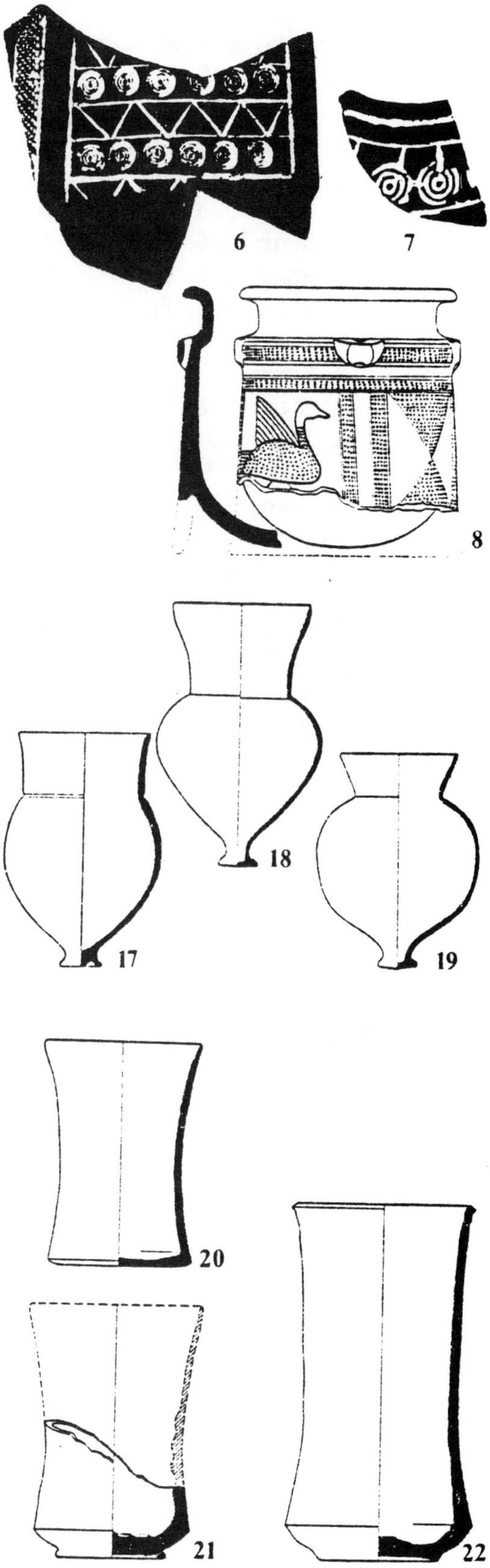

Plate VI

Nuzi (Temples E-A, Stratum II)

1. Starr:1938, Pl. 92:H (3:10)
2. Starr:1938, Pl. 92:M (3:10)
3. Starr:1938, Pl. 92:I (3:10)
4. Starr:1938, Pl. 77:B (3:10)
5. Starr:1938, Pl. 77:I (3:10)
6. Starr:1938. Pl. 77:C (3:10)
7. Starr:1938, Pl. 77:F (3:10)
8. Starr:1938, Pl. 77:G (3:10)
9. Starr:1938, Pl. 78:O (3:10)
10. Starr:1938, Pl. 78:E (3:10)
11. Starr:1938, Pl. 77:Q (3:10)
12. Starr:1938, Pl. 78:G (Stratum III) (3:10)
13. Starr:1938, Pl. 78:F (3:10)
14. Starr:1938, Pl. 78:I (3:10)

Comparisons

15. *UE* VII, Pl. 108:77 Ur, Old Babylonian (3:10)
16. *OIP* LXIII, Pl. 163:B.656.720 Khafaje, Old Babylonian (3:10)
17. Hrouda:1957, Tf. 8:20 Assur, Gruft 57 (3:8)
18. Hrouda:1957, Tf. 7:6 Assur, Gruft 9 (3:8)
19. Mallowan:1947, Pl. LXVII:15 Tell Brak, site H.H., level 1 (1:5)
20. Speiser:1933a, Pl. LX:4 Tell Billa, stratum 3 (3:10)
21. Speiser:1933a, Pl. LX:2 Tell Billa, stratum 3 (3:10)

Pl. VI

Yorgan Tepe (Nuzi)

Comparisons

Nuzi (Temples E-A, Stratum II)

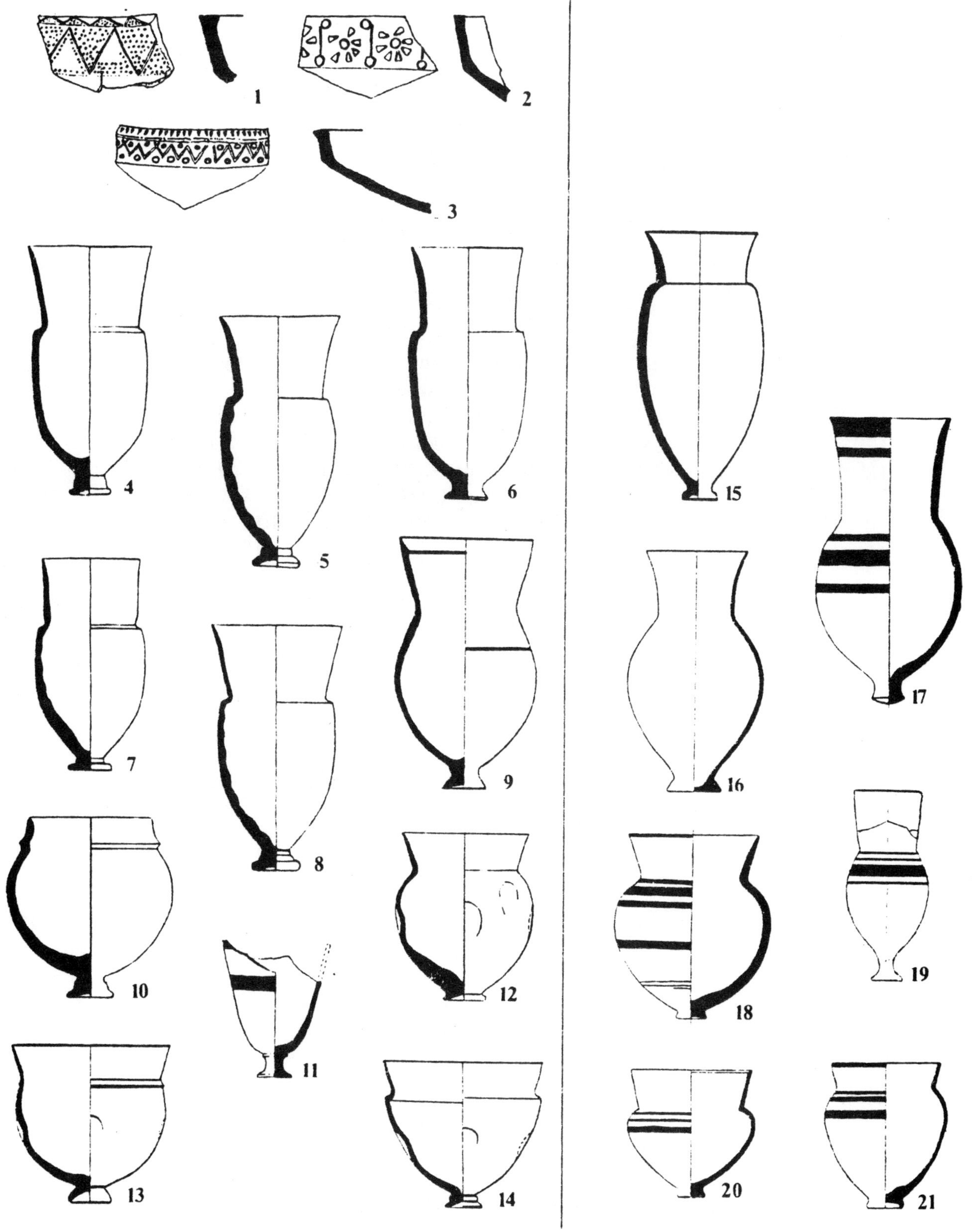

Plate VII

Nuzi (Temples E-A)

1. Starr:1938, Pl. 76:P (3:10)
2. Starr:1938, Pl. 76:K (3:10)
3. Starr:1938, Pl. 76:M (3:10)
4. Starr:1938, Pl. 76:S (3:10)
5. Starr:1938, Pl. 76:Z (3:10)
6. Starr:1938, Pl. 76:U (3:10)
7. Starr:1938, Pl. 76:W (3:10)
8. Starr:1938, Pl. 76:DD (3:10)
9. Starr:1938, Pl. 76:EE (3:10)
10. Starr:1938, Pl. 78:S (3:10)
11. Starr:1938, Pl. 78:R (3:10)
12. Starr:1938, Pl. 78:P (3:10)
13. Starr:1938, Pl. 78:Q (3:10)

Comparisons

14. *OIP* LXIII, Pl. 153:B.236.200b Ishchali, Late Larsa or Old Babylonian (3:10)
15. *OIP* LXIII, Pl. 153:B.237.200 Khafaje, Larsa Period (3:10)
16. *UE* II, Pl. 255:73 (=*UE* VIII:Pl. 40:34) Ur, ED II-Kassite Period (3:20)
17. Woolley:1955, Pl. CXVII, Type 93c Alalakh, levels V-III (3:20)
18. *OIP* LXXVIII, Pl. 95:17, Type 39B Nippur, level 56 E 1 (3:20)
19. *UE* VII, Pl. 108:76 Ur, Old Babylonian (3:10)
20. *OIP* LXIII, Pl. 153:B.247.700 Tell Asmar, Late Larsa (3:10)
21. Genouillac:1936, Pl. XXXIV:2426 Telloh, Ur III-Larsa (3:10)

Pl.VII

Yorgan Tepe (Nuzi)

Comparisons

Temples E-A

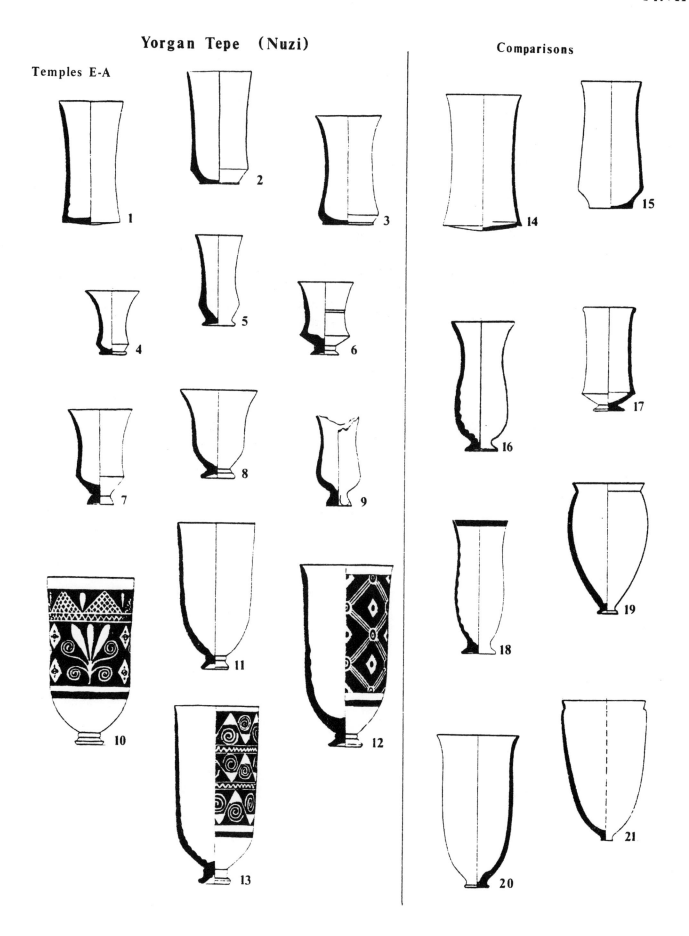

Plate VIII

Strata 5 and 4

1. Speiser:1933a, Pl. LV:4   (3:40)
2. Speiser:1933a, Pl. LVI:5   (3:10)
3. Speiser:1933a, Pl. LIX:2   (3:10)
4. Speiser:1933a, Pl. LIX:3   (3:10)
5. Speiser:1933a, Pl. LVIII:9   (3:20)
6. Speiser:1933a, Pl. LIX:1   (3:20)
7. Speiser:1933a, Pl. LIX:4   (3:20)

Comparisons

8. Hamlin:1974, Fig. II:1a   Dinkha Tepe, stratum 8   (1:5)
9. Hamlin:1974, Fig. II:1b   Dinkha Tepe, stratum 2c area 7   (1:5)
10. Mallowan:1937, Fig. 23:1 Chagar Bazar, Intermediate level 1   (3:10)
11. Mallowan:1937, Fig. 16:8 Chagar Bazar, Early Intermediate level   (3:10)
12. Mallowan:1936, Fig. 17:14 Chagar Bazar, level 1   (3:10)
13. Mallowan:1936, Fig. 17:11 Chagar Bazar, level 1   (3:10)

Pl. VIII

Tell Billa

Comparisons

Stratum 5

Stratum 4

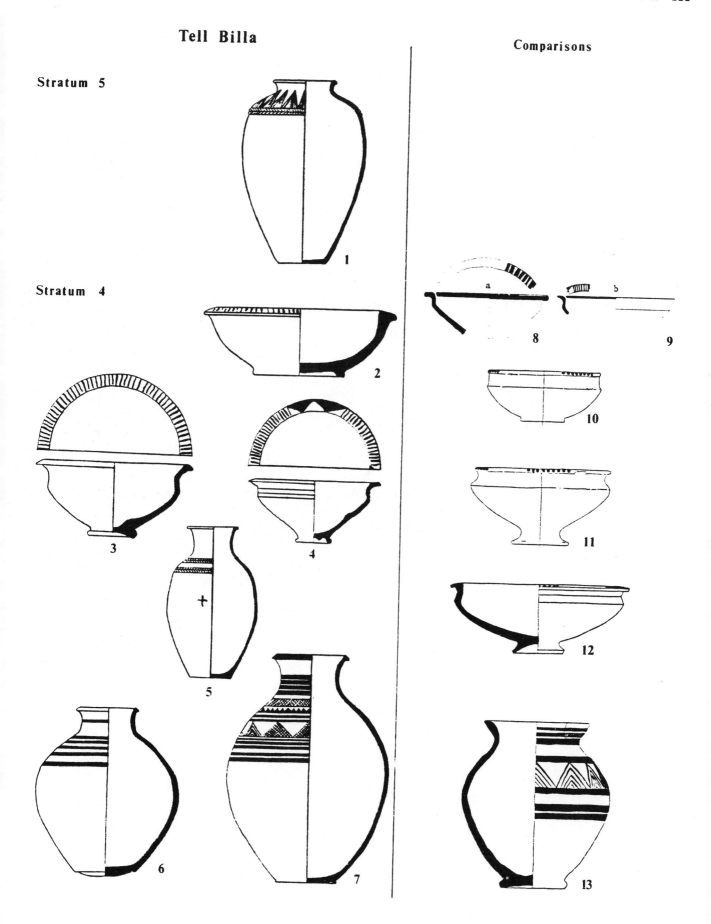

Plate IX

Stratum 4

1. Speiser:1933a, Pl. LVII:5 (3:40)
2. Speiser:1933a, Pl. LIX:5 (3:10)
3. Speiser:1933a, Pl. LVII:2 (3:10)

Comparisons

4. *OIP* LXIII, Pl. 153:B.236.300 Tell Asmar, Late Larsa (3:10)
5. *UE* II, Pl. 255:72 Ur, ED II (3:20)
6. *OIP* LXIII, Pl. 184:C.548.720 Tell Asmar, Late Larsa (3:20)
7. *OIP* LXIII, Pl. 166:B.788.320 Ishchali, Late Larsa or Old Babylonian (3:10)

Stratum 3

8. Speiser:1933a, Pl. LX:5 (3:10)
9. Speiser:1933a, Pl. LX:4 (3:10)
10. Speiser:1933a, Pl. LX:3 (3:10)
11. Speiser:1933a, Pl. LX:2 (3:10)
12. Speiser:1933a, Pl. LXII:5 (3:10)
13. Speiser:1933a, Pl. LXII:7 (3:10)
14. Speiser:1933a, Pl. LXII:4 (3:10)
15. Speiser:1933a, Pl. LXI:5 (3:10)
16. Speiser:1933a, Pl. LXI:4 (3:10)
17. Speiser:1933a, Pl. LXI:3 (3:10)

Comparisons

18. *OIP* LXXVIII, Pl. 95:4 Nippur, level TA. 1 (Old Babylonian) (3:10)
19. Mallowan:1936, Fig. 17:4 Chagar Bazar, level 1 (3:10)
20. *OIP* LXIII, Pl. 153:B.236.200c Tell Asmar, Late Larsa (3:10)
21. Hrouda:1957, Tf. 7:6 Assur, Gruft 9 (3:8)
22. *OIP* LXIII, Pl. 153:B.247.700 Tell Asmar, Late Larsa (3:10)
23. *OIP* LXIII, Pl. 153:B.237.100 Tell Asmar, Late Larsa (3:10)

Pl. IX

Tell Billa

Stratum 4

Comparisons

Stratum 3

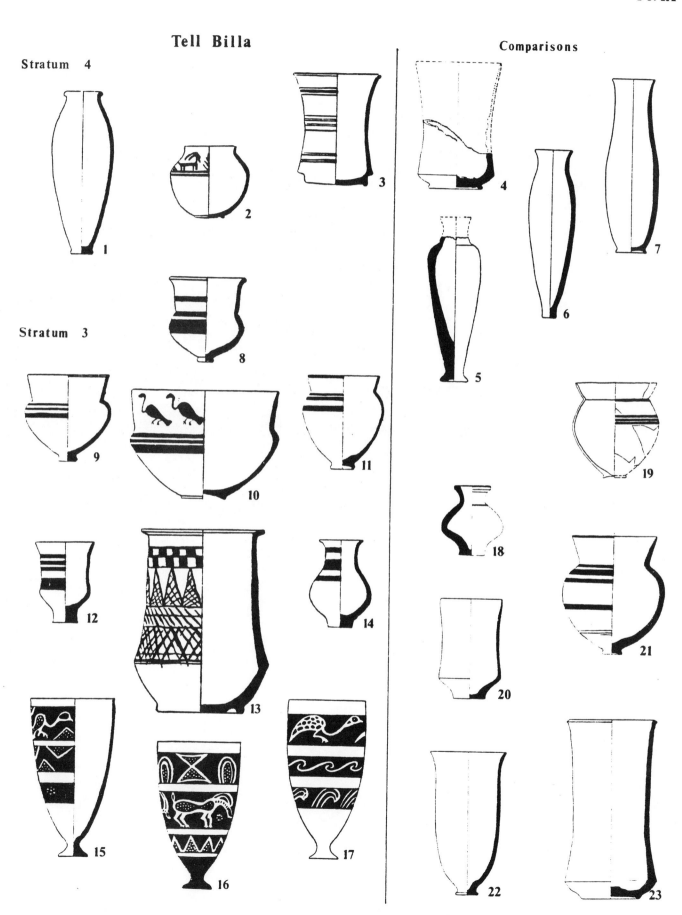

Plate X

Sargonid

    1. Mallowan: 1947, Pl. LXV:13 (3:20)
    2. Mallowan: 1947, Pl. LXV:15 (3:20)
    3. Mallowan: 1947, Pl. LXV:1 (3:20)
    4. Mallowan: 1947, Pl. LXV:4 (3:20)
    5. Mallowan: 1947, Pl. LXV:8 (3:20)
    6. Mallowan: 1947, Pl. LXIX:2 (3:20)

Comparisons

    7. Speiser: 1935, Pl. LXXI:161 Tepe Gawra, stratum V (3:20)
    8. Speiser: 1935, Pl. LXIX:137 Tepe Gawra, stratum VI (3:20)

Ur III

    9. Mallowan: 1947, Pl. LXXV:15 (3:10)
   10. Mallowan: 1947, Pl. LXXV:16 (3:10)
   11. Mallowan: 1947, Pl. LXXV:17 (3:10)

Second Millennium B.C.

Site E.R.

   12. Mallowan: 1947, Pl. LXXIII:5 (3:10)

Comparison

   13. Mallowan: 1936, Fig. 14:13 Chagar Bazar, level 1 (3:20)

Pl. X

Tell Brak

Comparisons

Sargonid

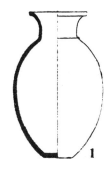

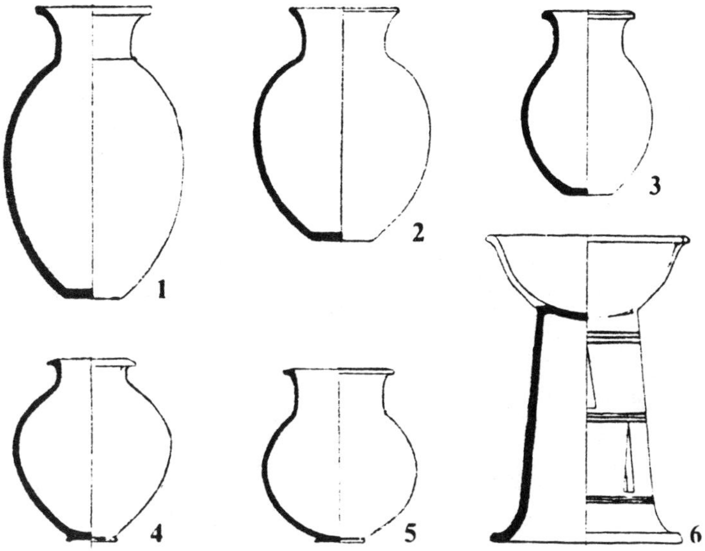

1

2

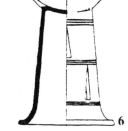

3

4

5

6

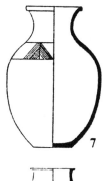

7

8

Ur III

9

10

11

Second Millennium B.C.

Site E.R.

12

13

Plate XI

Site H.H.

Level 3

1. Mallowan:1947, Pl. LXVII:19   (1:5)
2. Mallowan:1947, Pl. LXXVIII:5   (3:8)
3. Mallowan:1947, Pl. LXXVIII:9   (3:8)
4. Mallowan:1947, Pl. LXXVIII:6   (3:8)
5. Mallowan:1947, Pl. LXXVIII:8   (3:8)
6. Mallowan:1947, Pl. LXXVIII:13   (3:8)
7. Mallowan:1947, Pl. LXXVIII:12   (3:8)
8. Mallowan:1947, Pl. LXXVIII:11   (3:8)

Comparisons

9. Woolley:1955, Pl. XCV AT/39/279, Type 93c Alalakh, level V *
10. Speiser:1933a, Pl. LXXII Tell Billa, stratum 4 *
11. Woolley:1955, Pl. XCV AT/46/275 Alalakh, level V *
12. Woolley:1955, Pl. XCV AT/46/336 Alalakh, level V *
13. Woolley:1955, Pl. XCIVa Alalakh, level VI **
14. Woolley:1955, Pl. XCV AT/46/272 Alalakh, level V *

*72% of Woolley and Speiser

**25% of Woolley

Pl. XI

Tell Brak

Comparisons

Site H.H.

Level 3

1

9

2

3

10

4

11

5

6

12

13

7

8

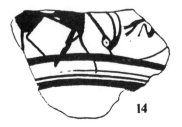

14

Plate XII

Site H.H.

Level 2
1. Mallowan:1947, Pl. LXXVII:1   (3:10)
2. Mallowan:1947, Pl. LXXVII:3   (3:10)
3. Mallowan:1947, Pl. LXXVII:2   (3:10)
4. Mallowan:1947, Pl. LXXVII:5   (3:10)
5. Mallowan:1947, Pl. LXXVII:7   (3:10)
6. Mallowan:1947, Pl. LXXVII:4   (3:10)
7. Mallowan:1947, Pl. LXXVII:8   (3:10)
8. Mallowan:1947, Pl. LXXVII:9   (3:10)
9. Mallowan:1947, Pl. LXXVII:6   (3:10)

Comparisons
10. Mallowan:1946, Fig. 11:8   Jidle, level 3   (3:10)
11. Mallowan:1946, Fig. 11:6   Jidle, level 2   (3:10)
12. Mallowan:1946, Fig. 11:10 Jidle, level 2   (3:10)
13. Speiser:1933a, Pl. LXI:2 Tell Billa, stratum 3   (3:10)
14. Speiser:1933a, Pl. LXI:1 Tell Billa, stratum 3   (3:10)
15. Starr:1938, Pl. 69:A_2 Nuzi, stratum II   (1:5)
16. Hrouda:1957, Tf. 3:3 Assur   (3:8)
17. Hrouda:1957, Tf. 1:4 Assur, Grab 600   (3:8)

Pl. XII

Tell Brak

Comparisons

Level 2

1

2

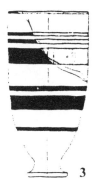

3

4

10

11

5

6

7

8

9

12

13

14

15

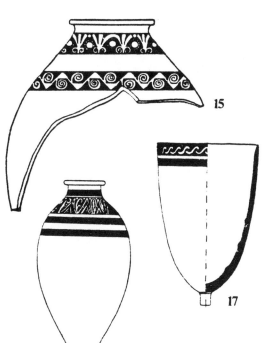

16

17

Plate XIII

Site H.H.
  Level 1
     1. Mallowan:1947, Pl. LXVII:14   (1:5)
     2. Mallowan:1947, Pl. LXVII:15   (1:5)
     3. Mallowan:1947, Pl. LXVII:16   (1:5)
     4. Mallowan:1947, Pl. LXVII:21   (1:5)
     5. Mallowan:1947, Pl. LXVII:20   (1:5)
     6. Mallowan:1947, Pl. LXXIX:2   (3:8)
     7. Mallowan:1947, Pl. LXXIX:3   (3:8)
     8. Mallowan:1947, Pl. LXXIX:1   (3:8)
Comparisons
     9. *OIP* LXIII, Pl. 160:B.556.720 Khafaje, Old Babylonian   (3:10)
    10. Starr:1938, Pl. 78:0 Nuzi, stratum II   (3:10)
    11. Hrouda:1957, Tf. 8:20 Assur, Gruft 57   (3:8)
    12. Woolley:1955, Pl. CXVII, Type 94b Alalakh, levels VII-II
                                     (most common in level IV)   (3:20)
    13. Woolley:1955, Pl. CXVII, Type 94a Alalakh, levels V-II
                                     (most common in level IV)   (3:20)
    14. Genouillac:1936, Pl. XXXIV:2426 Telloh   (3:10)
    15. Woolley:1955, Pl. CXX, Type 118b Alalakh, levels V-II
                                 (most common in levels IV-III)   (3:20)

Pl. XIII

Tell Brak

Comparisons

Level 1

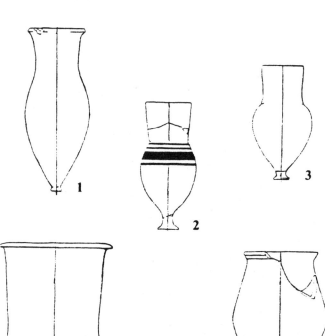

1

2

3

4

5

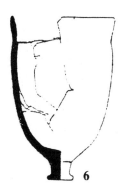

7

6

8

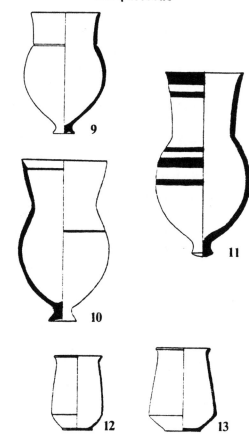

9

10

11

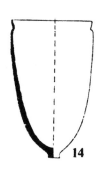

12

13

14

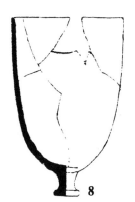

15

Plate XIV

Levels XVII-VIII
    1. Woolley:1955, Pl. XCI:ATP/47/107 (level XII) *
    2. Woolley:1955, Pl. XCI:ATP/47/149 (level XIIb) (3:10)
    3. Woolley:1955, Pl. XCI:ATP/47/150 (level XII) (3:10)
    4. Woolley:1955, Pl. XC:ATP/47/174 (level XII) *

Level VII
    5. Woolley:1955, Pl. CXX:Type 118a (3:20)
    6. Woolley:1955, Pl. CXVII:Type 94b (3:20)
Comparisons
    7. *OIP* LXXVIII, Pl. 94:5, Type 35 Nippur, Old Babylonian (3:10)
    8. Starr:1938, Pl. 76:C Nuzi, stratum II (3:10)
    9. Speiser:1933a, Pl. LX:1 Tell Billa, stratum 3 (3:10)
    10. Starr:1938, Pl. 76:K Nuzi, stratum II (3:10)

Level VI
    11. Woolley:1955, Pl. XCIVa *
Comparisons
    12. Speiser:1933a, Pl. LXI:3 Tell Billa, stratum 3 (3:10)
    13. Mallowan:1947, Pl. LXXVII:5 Tell Brak, site H.H.; level 2 (3:10)
    14. Speiser:1933a, Pl. LXI:5 Tell Billa, stratum 3 (3:10)

*72% of Woolley

Pl. XIV

Tell Atchana (Alalakh)

Comparisons

Levels XVII—VIII

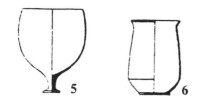

1

2

3

4

Level VII

5

6

7

8

9

10

Level VI

11

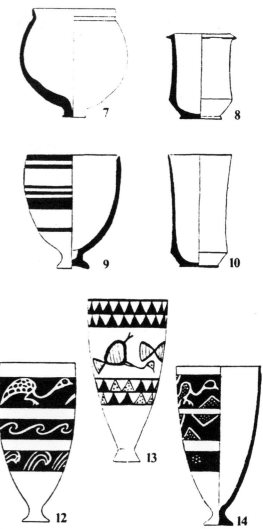

12

13

14

Plate XV

Level V
1. Woolley:1955, Pl. CI:AT/46/266 *
2. Woolley:1955, Pl, CI:AT/46/266 *
3. Woolley:1955, Pl. CI:AT/46/266 *
4. Woolley:1955, Pl. CI:AT/46/266 *
5. Woolley:1955, P. XCV *
6. Woolley:1955, Pl. CXVII:Type 94a (3:20)
7. Woolley:1955, Pl. CXX:Type 124 (3:10)

Comparisons
8. Özgüc:1953, Abb. 26 Kültepe, Kaniš Karum 1b (3:20)
9. Özgüc:1953, Abb. 25 Kültepe, Kaniš Karum 1b (3:20)
10. Speiser:1933a, Pl. LX:4 Tell Billa, stratum 3 (3:10)
11. Speiser:1933a, Pl. LX:6 Tell Billa, stratum 3 (3:10)
12. Hrouda:1957, Tf. 7:6 Assur, Gruft 9 (3:8)

Level IV
13. Woolley:1955, Pl. CV:ATP/343 **
14. Woolley:1955, Pl. CV:ATP/8/143 **
15. Woolley:1955, Pl. CXX:Type 118a (3:20)
16. Woolley:1955, Pl. CVI:ATP/8/72 **
17. Woolley:1955, Pl. CVI:ATP/37/277 **
18. Woolley:1955, Pl. CII:b ATP/38/18 **

Comparisons
19. Mallowan:1947, Pl. LXXXI:6 Chagar Bazar, level 1E (3:10)
20. Hrouda:1957, Tf. 8:4 Assur (3:20)
21. Speiser:1935, Pl. LXXIII:194 Tepe Gawra, stratum IV (3:20)

*72% of Woolley

**72% of Cecchini:1965 nos. 254, 257, 263, 264, 233 respectively

Pl. XV

Tell Atchana (Alalakh)

Comparisons

Level V

1   2   3

4

5

6

7

8   9

10   11

12

Level IV

13   14   15

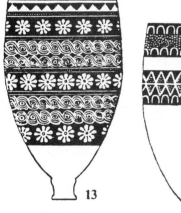

16   17   18

19

20   21

STYLE SHEET
UNDENA PUBLICATIONS

General Procedures

MANUSCRIPTS: Keep a duplicate copy of your submitted manuscript since this will not be included when proofs are sent to you.

PROOFS: Each author will receive proofs for corrections.

CORRECTIONS and CHANGES: Corrections and changes must be kept to an absolute minimum. Major changes, i.e. changes that affect more than a couple of lines, or a great many minor changes, will be at the author's expense, and subject to a $1.20 per change surcharge. All changes as submitted by the author on the proofs are suggestions only and may be disregarded at the discretion of the editor. Changes that affect entire pages will not be accepted.

COPIES: Besides 10 complimentary copies of the work, authors may take advantage of a one-time prepublication discount of 40% (plus postage and handling). Additional copies are available in unlimited quantity at 20% discount (plus postage and handling).

Manuscript Preparation

MANUSCRIPT: All material must be typed, double-spaced throughout on *non*-erasable and *non*-onionskin bond; photocopies are accepted. Isolated corrections may be entered by hand, but should be printed. The University of Chicago Press *Manual of Style* is recommended as a guide to style.

FOOTNOTES: All notes are to be typed, double-spaced, on separate pages with running numeration.

ABSTRACT: All manuscripts should be accompanied by an abstract of approximately 100-125 words.

TABLES and CHARTS: Tables and charts must be laid out as desired to appear in print, with explanations in the margin when the typed manuscript does not show clearly the intended format.

TITLES: Authors are strongly encouraged to divide their manuscripts into sections, subsections, etc., numbered and titled. There should be a table of contents (following the abstract) referring to these sections on the following model:
>   1. (Major heading)
>   1.1. (Sub-heading)
>   1.2. (Sub-heading)
>   1.2.1. (Second level sub-heading)
>   1.2.2. (Second level sub-heading)
>   2. (Major heading)

REFERENCES and BIBLIOGRAPHY: For all references please include (a) *Full* name of author(s), (b) place of publication *and* name of publisher, (c) page numbers of article.

UNDERSCORES:
Straight underline for *italics*: _____
Wavy underline for **bold face**: ~~~~~~~
Wavy and straight underline for ***bold italics***: _____
Double underline for SMALL CAPS: =======
Triple underline for REGULAR CAPS: _____

SYRO-MESOPOTAMIAN STUDIES

A journal devoted to the study of the civilizations of ancient Iraq and Syria from late prehistory to the First Millennium B.C.—providing an outlet for the publication of primary sources and a forum for the archaeological, historical and linguistic analysis of pertinent phenomena.

Editor: M. Kelly-Buccellati
Associate Editor: O. Rouault
Assistant Editor: W. Shelby
Advisory Board: J. Bottéro, I. J. Gelb, G. Gullini, Th. Jacobsen, M. Van Loon